# The Big Book of Jams and Jellies

200 Fun and Delicious Artisan Homemade Jams & Jellies Recipes for Anyone

Brendan Fawn

3

# Introduction

When we talk about jams and jellies we always imagine something sweet, pleasant and fragrant. For me, jam is associated with the summer. When I hear the word jam, I see colorful pictures of summer and a lot of sun.

Jam could be prepared from any fruits or berries - both traditional as apples, strawberries, raspberries, gooseberries or pears, and exotic ones, for example, mango, pineapple, bananas or papaya. Some fans of unusual sweet desserts prepare jams and jellies from carrots, tomatoes, cucumbers, oranges, chestnuts or walnuts.

Jams can have different forms, colors, and tastes. Jams and jellies can be liquid and thick, sour, very sweet or with a hint of sweetness or sourness. We can cook them with the sugar, honey, stevia or erythritol. Jams have orange, red, purple, pink, dark blue and many other colors.

In this cookbook, you will find traditional, homemade apple, strawberry, raspberry, gooseberry jams, and jellies, but also few exotic ones with coconuts or oranges. Everyone will find tasty jams or jellies for himself.

Moreover, you don't need to be a professional 28 Michelin Star chef to cook sweet and mouthwatering jams and jellies from this cookbook and to prepare tasty fruit desserts for yourself, your friends and family. I would like to encourage you to test these artisan jams and jellies recipes and to experiment with the ingredients adding your own flavors!

# Jams & Jellies – Sunny Harvest

Summer is the time when we can enjoy sweet and colorful fruits, but what about winter? How to preserve those sunny days and sweet tastes? People invented jams and jellies. Delicious and fragrant jam or jelly, with the taste and smell of the sun and heat, is especially pleasant to taste during the cold winter period, recalling the hot and sunny summer. Moreover, family tea is hard to imagine without the fragrant and sweet raspberry jam or blackcurrant jelly, which is loved by both children and adults. Tea with a tempting sweet jam dessert brings people together, provides an opportunity to socialize, communicate and enjoy delicious fruit desserts.

Jams and jellies are preserving the taste of natural berries and fruits, but what is more, sweet fruit desserts improve mood and give a piece of summer and summer heat. Fruit jams also fill us with energy and vitality and are healthy, because they contain various vitamins, minerals, and trace elements.

Each housewife has her own secrets of how to prepare delicious redcurrant, blackcurrant, strawberry, raspberry, apple, pear, quince, gooseberry, sweet cherry jam, peach jam.

There are many ways to process the fruits to cook delicious jellies or jams, among which everyone can choose the right one. However, there are general cooking rules and some subtleties how to prepare tasty jams that every housewife should know, no matter what jam recipes she uses.

From this cookbook, you will learn how to prepare classic homemade jams and jellies, which will be mouthwatering and delicious. Enjoy!

# Orange-Strawberry Jam

---

### Prep Time: 30 min. | Makes around 7 12 oz jars

---

## Ingredients:

5 lb fresh, small strawberries

2 oranges, peeled and diced

1 tbsp. orange zest, minced

5 cups of brown sugar

5 tbsp. orange juice

## How to Prepare:

1. In a saucepan, combine the strawberries and orange cubes and spoon the sugar over the fruits. Leave the strawberries for at least few hours unrefrigerated at room temperature.

2. Boil the strawberries and oranges over medium heat for around 30 minutes, stirring all the time with a spoon until the sugar dissolves but don't crush the berries or orange. Remove the foam from the strawberry jam.

3.  10 min. before the jam is ready stir in the orange zest and pour some orange juice and keep stirring until the strawberries and orange mixture has gelled enough. Spoon some jam on a plate and wait until thickened, if not continue boiling and testing every 5 minutes.

4.  Remove the saucepan with the strawberries from the heat and ladle freshly cooked jam into sterilized jars up to 1/5 inch from the top.

5.  Flip the jars with the orange-strawberry jam upside down or boil for around 10 minutes and then leave to cool. Check the lids by pressing them with the finger. In case some of the jars with the jam are unsealed, place them into the fridge or reprocess the unsealed jars.

Nutritional Information (1 tbsp):

Calories: 52; Total fat: 4 oz; Total carbohydrates: 7 oz; Protein: 3 oz

# Kiwi-Pineapple Jam

***Prep Time: 40 min.*** | ***Makes around 6-7 10 oz jars***

## Ingredients:

2 lb kiwis, peeled and diced

1 big pineapple, peeled and diced

1 tbsp. gelatin

5 cups of sugar

3 tsp. vanilla

## How to Prepare:

1. In a big pot, combine the kiwis, pineapple cubes, sugar, gelatin and vanilla and boil over medium heat for around 40 minutes, stirring all the time until the sugar dissolves. Remove the foam and the scum from the jam.

2. Spoon some jam on a plate and wait until gelled. Check by pressing with the finger or the spoon, if not gelled enough continue boiling and testing every 5-10 minutes until gelled.

3.  When the jam is ready, remove the pot with the fruits from the heat and pour the freshly cooked jam into the sterilized and hot jars up to 1/4 inch from the top.

4.  Seal the jars and flip them upside down or boil them for around 10 minutes and then leave to cool. Check the lids by pressing them with the finger. In case some of the jars with the kiwi-pineapple jam are unsealed, place them into the fridge or reprocess the unsealed jars.

Nutritional Information (1 tbsp):
Calories: 70; Total fat: 8 oz; Total carbohydrates: 13 oz; Protein: 5 oz

# Blackberry-Orange Jelly

---

*Prep Time: 1 hour | Makes: 8 10 oz jars*

---

Ingredients:

3 lbs blackberries

4 oranges, peeled and diced

5 cups of sugar

2 tsp. citric acid

How to Prepare:

1. Spoon 1 cup of the sugar over the berries and oranges. Set aside for overnight.

2. Boil the blackberries and oranges over the low heat for around 30 minutes, stirring all the time. Pour in some water. Then mash the berries with the potato masher and strain the mixture to get 4-5 cups of the juice.

3. In a saucepan, combine the juice with the remaining sugar and boil the juice for 30 minutes until thickened. The jelly should be thick enough to pour it into the jars. Skim the foam from the surface. 10 minutes before the jelly is ready mix in the citric acid.

4. Remove the saucepan from the heat and pour the freshly cooked jelly into the sterilized jars.

5. Turn the jars upside down or boil for around 10 minutes and then leave to cool. Check the lids by pressing them with the finger. In case some of the jars with the jelly are unsealed, place them into the fridge or reprocess the unsealed jars.

Nutritional Information (1 tbsp):

Calories: 52; Total fat: 5 oz; Total carbohydrates: 9 oz; Protein: 4 oz

# Rose Petal & Goosberry Jelly

*Prep Time: 50 min.* | *Makes: 6-7 11 oz jars*

Ingredients:

45 oz gooseberries, fresh

5 oz fresh rose petals

5 cups of sugar

2 tbsp. pure vanilla extract

1 tbsp. citric acid or lemon juice

How to Prepare:

1. Spoon 4 tbsp. sugar over the gooseberries and set aside for few hours. Then mash the berries using the potato masher.

2. In a pan, heat the water and boil the rose petals on a low heat for about 15 minutes.

3. Pour some water and boil the berries over the low heat for around 15-20 minutes, stirring all the time. Then strain the gooseberries to get 4 cups juice.

4. In a saucepan, combine the juice with the sugar and rose petals. Boil the juice for 30 minutes. The jelly should be thick enough to pour it into the jars. Add the vanilla and citric acid.

5. Remove the saucepan from the heat and ladle the freshly cooked jelly into the sterilized jars and seal the jars.

6. Flip the jars upside down or boil for around 10 minutes and then leave to cool. Check the lids by pressing them with the finger. In case some of the jars with the rose petal jelly are unsealed, place them into the fridge or reprocess the unsealed jars.

**Nutritional Information (1 tbsp):**

Calories: 55; Total fat: 4 oz; Total carbohydrates: 10 oz; Protein: 4 oz

# Kiwi-Strawberry Jam

---

***Prep Time: 30 min.*** | ***Makes around 7 12 oz jars***

---

Ingredients:

6 lb fresh, small strawberries

2 kiwis, cut into rings

1 tsp. orange zest, minced

6 cups of sugar

2 tbsp. orange juice

How to Prepare:

1.  In a saucepan, combine the strawberries and kiwis and spoon the sugar over the fruits. Leave the strawberries for at least few hours unrefrigerated at room temperature.

2.  Boil the strawberries and kiwis over the medium heat for around 30 minutes, stirring all the time with a spoon until the sugar dissolves, but don't crush the berries nor kiwis. Skim the foam from the orange jam.

3.  Few minutes before the orange jam is ready, stir in the orange zest and orange juice and keep stirring until the strawberries mixture has gelled enough. Then place some jam on a plate and wait until thickened, check by pressing with the finger or the spoon. Continue boiling and testing every 5 minutes until the jam will get thick enough to ladle it into the jars.

4.  Remove the saucepan with the strawberries and kiwis from the heat and ladle freshly cooked jam into hot and sterilized jars up to 1/5 inch from the top.

5.  Flip the jars with the strawberry jam upside down or boil for around 10 minutes and then leave to cool. Check the lids by pressing them with the finger. In case some of the jars with the strawberry jam are unsealed, place them into the fridge or reprocess the unsealed jars.

Nutritional Information (1 tbsp):
Calories: 55; Total fat: 3 oz; Total carbohydrates: 8 oz; Protein: 2 oz

# Orange Taste Pineapple & Strawberry Jam

---

### *Prep Time: 40 min. | Makes around 7 10 oz jars*

---

Ingredients:

8 cups of small strawberries

2 cups of pineapple cubes

6 cups of sugar

2 tsp. pure orange extract

2 tbsp. orange juice


How to Prepare:

1. In a saucepan, combine the strawberries and pineapple cubes and spoon the sugar over the fruits.

2. Boil the strawberries with the pineapple slices over the medium heat for around 40 minutes, stirring until the sugar dissolves, but don't crush the berries nor pineapple cubes. Skim the foam from the pineapple strawberry jam.

3. 5-10 minutes before the pineapple strawberry jam is ready, stir in the orange juice and orange extract. Keep stirring until the strawberries and pineapple mixture has gelled enough. Continue boiling and testing every 5 minutes until the jam will get thick enough to ladle it into the jars.

4. Remove the saucepan with the strawberries and pineapple cubes from the heat and ladle freshly cooked jam into the hot and sterilized jars up to 1/4 inch from the top.

5. Flip the jars with the pineapple strawberry jam upside down or boil for around 10 minutes and then leave to cool. Check the lids by pressing them with the finger. In case some of the jars with the pineapple strawberry jam are unsealed, place them into the fridge or reprocess the unsealed jars.

Nutritional Information (1 tbsp):

Calories: 50; Total fat: 1 oz; Total carbohydrates: 23 oz; Protein: 7 oz

# Gooseberry Jam with Peanuts

*Prep Time: 50 min.│ Makes: 7-8 10 oz jars*

Ingredients:

2 lb gooseberries

1 cup of peanuts

4 cups of brown sugar

3 tbsp. lemon juice, squeezed

2 tsp. vanilla

How to Prepare:

1. Preheat the oven to 300°-350° Fahrenheit and bake the peanuts on a low heat for around 10 minutes. Then grind the peanuts. In a bowl, combine the sugar with the vanilla and mix well.

2. Then place the gooseberries into a big saucepan and spoon the sugar-vanilla mixture on top and leave for at least 6 hours unrefrigerated at room temperature or place in the fridge overnight.

3. In the same saucepan boil the gooseberries and sugar-vanilla mixture over high heat for around 10 minutes, stirring all the time with a spoon until sugar dissolves.

4. Then reduce the heat and continue to boil for around 40 minutes but don't forget to skim the foam from the berries.

5. Pour the lemon juice and add the nuts. Keep stirring until the berries mixture has gelled and thickened.

6. Remove the saucepan with the gooseberries from the heat and pour the freshly cooked jam into the sterilized jars up to 1/5 inch from the top.

7. Seal the jars and then turn the jars upside down. Leave them for overnight to cool completely and only then turn them back.

**Nutritional Information (1 tbsp):**

Calories: 68; Total fat: 3 oz; Total carbohydrates: 8 oz; Protein: 2 oz

# Cinnamon Strawberry Jam

*Prep Time: 50 min.* | *Makes: 7-8 10 oz jars*

## Ingredients:

5 lb fresh strawberries

6 cups of sugar

2 tsp. cinnamon

## How to Prepare:

1. Place the strawberries into a big saucepan and spoon the sugar on top. Then sprinkle the cinnamon and leave for at least 6 hours unrefrigerated at room temperature or place in the fridge overnight.

2. In the same saucepan boil the strawberries and sugar-vanilla mixture over high heat for around 10 minutes, stirring all the time with a spoon until sugar dissolves.

3. Then reduce the heat and continue to boil for around 40 minutes but don't forget to skim the foam from the strawberries.

4. Pour the lemon juice and keep stirring until the strawberries mixture has gelled and thickened.

5. Remove the saucepan with the strawberries from the heat and pour freshly cooked jam into sterilized jars up to 1/5 inch from the top.

6. Seal the jars and then turn the jars upside down. Leave them for overnight to cool completely and only then turn them back.

7. Or you can do it more traditionally by placing the jars into the water bath and boiling for around 7-10 minutes and then leaving to cool. Check the lids by pressing them with the finger. In case some of the jars with the strawberry jam are unsealed, place them into the fridge or reprocess the unsealed jars.

## Nutritional Information (1 tbsp):

Calories: 69; Total fat: 2 oz; Total carbohydrates: 3 oz; Protein: 0.7 oz

# Lime-Strawberry Jam

**Prep Time: 50 min. | Makes: 9-10 8 oz jars**

## Ingredients:

4 lb fresh and sweet strawberries

5 limes, peeled and diced

4 cups of sugar

1 tsp. vanilla

## How to Prepare:

1. Spoon 2 cups of the sugar over the diced limes. Leave for at least 3 hours unrefrigerated at room temperature or place in the fridge overnight. Place the strawberries into a big saucepan and boil with the remaining sugar and limes.

2. Boil the strawberries mixture over medium heat for around 30 minutes, stirring all the time until the sugar dissolves. Remove the foam from the strawberries jam while boiling. Keep stirring until the strawberries jam has gelled.

3. Remove the saucepan with the strawberries from the heat and pour freshly cooked jam into sterilized jars up to 1/5 inch from the top.

4. Seal the jars and then turn the jars upside down. Leave them for overnight to cool completely and only then turn them back. Check the lids by pressing them with the

finger. In case some of the jars with the strawberry jam are unsealed, place them into the fridge or reprocess the unsealed jars.

**Nutritional Information (1 tbsp):**

Calories: 50; Total fat: 4 oz; Total carbohydrates: 3 oz; Protein: 2 oz

# Cherry-Redcurrant Jelly

---

*Prep Time: 50 min.* | *Makes: 6-7 11 oz jars*

---

## Ingredients:

6 cups of redcurrants, fresh

2 cups of sweet cherry syrup

5 cups of sugar

1 tbsp. pure vanilla extract

## How to Prepare:

1. Spoon 4 tbsp. sugar over the redcurrants and set aside for few hours and then mash the berries with the potato masher.

2. Pour some water and boil the redcurrants over the low heat for around 15-20 minutes, stirring all the time. Then strain the redcurrants to get 4 cups of the juice.

3. In a saucepan, combine the juice with the cherry syrup and sugar and boil the juice for 30 minutes. The jelly should be thick enough to ladle it into the jars. If not, add more sugar. Remove the foam from the surface.

4. Remove the saucepan from the heat and ladle the freshly cooked jelly into the sterilized jars and seal the jars.

5. Flip the jars upside down or boil for around 10 minutes and then leave to cool. Check the lids by pressing them with the finger. In case some of the jars with the redcurrant jelly are unsealed, place them into the fridge or reprocess the unsealed jars.

## Nutritional Information (1 tbsp):

Calories: 54; Total fat: 2 oz; Total carbohydrates: 9 oz; Protein: 3 oz

# Orange & Raspberry Jam

---

### *Prep Time: 40 min.* | *Makes: 5-6 11 oz jars*

---

Ingredients:

3 lb fresh and sweet raspberries

2 oranges, diced

2 tbsp. orange zest, minced

5 cups of sugar

3 tbsp. orange juice, freshly squeezed

How to Prepare:

1. Spoon the raspberries into a food processor or blender and lightly puree them to have halves of the berries.
2. In a large saucepan, combine the raspberries, oranges and sugar and boil over the medium heat for around 40 minutes, stirring all the time with a spoon until the sugar dissolves. Take a big spoon and skim the foam from the raspberry jam.

3. Spoon some jam on a plate and wait until thickened, if not continue boiling and testing. The jam should be thick enough to spoon it into jars. Few minutes before the jam is ready stir in the orange juice and orange zest and keep stirring until the raspberries mixture has thickened.

4. When the jam is ready, remove the saucepan with the raspberries from the heat and spoon freshly cooked jam into sterilized jars up to 1/5 inch from the top.

5. Seal the jars and then process them in a water bath. In a large pot, boil the jars for around 10 minutes and then take them out and leave to cool. Check the lids by pressing them with the finger. In case some of the jars with the raspberry jam are unsealed, place them into the fridge or reprocess the unsealed jars.

Nutritional Information (1 tbsp):
Calories: 72; Total fat: 0.2 oz; Total carbohydrates: 2.8 oz; Protein: 0 oz

# Wild Cherry Jelly

---

*Prep Time: 1 hour│Makes: 8-10 10 oz jars*

---

## Ingredients:

4 lbs wild cherries, pitted

5 cups of sugar

2 tsp. citric acid

## How to Prepare:

1.  Spoon 1 cup of sugar over the berries and set aside for overnight.

2.  Pour some water and boil the berries over the low heat for around 30 minutes, stirring all the time. Then mash the berries with the potato masher and strain the mixture to get 4-5 cups of the juice.

3.  In a saucepan, combine the juice with the remaining sugar and boil the juice for 30 minutes until thickened. The jelly should be thick enough to pour it into the jars. Skim the foam from the surface. 10 minutes before the jelly is ready mix in the citric acid.

4.  Remove the saucepan from the heat and pour the freshly cooked jelly into the sterilized jars.

5.  Turn the jars upside down or boil for around 10 minutes and then leave to cool. Check the lids by pressing them with the finger. In case some of the jars with the wild cherry jelly are unsealed, place them into the fridge or reprocess the unsealed jars.

## Nutritional Information (1 tbsp):

Calories: 57; Total fat: 4 oz; Total carbohydrates: 8 oz; Protein: 3 oz

# Strawberry Peach Jam

*Prep Time: 40 min.* | *Makes: 5-6 11 oz jars*

Ingredients:

2.5 lb peaches, washed and sliced

2 lb small strawberries

5 cups of sugar

1 tbsp. lemon juice or 1 tsp. citric acid

How to Prepare:

1. In a big pot, combine the sliced peaches with the strawberries and add the sugar on top. Leave for 5 hours unrefrigerated at room temperature.

2. Boil the fruits with the sugar for 40 minutes, stirring until the sugar dissolves. Take a big spoon and remove the foam from the jam surface.

3. 5 minutes before the jam is ready mix in the lemon juice or citric acid and keep stirring until the jam has thickened.

4. Spoon the freshly cooked peach jam into sterilized jars up to 1/5 inch from the top and then seal the jars.

5. Now turn the jars upside down and leave them for at least 5 hours or for overnight to cool completely and only then turn them back. Check the lids by pressing them with the finger. In case some of the jars with the strawberry peach jam are unsealed, place them into the fridge or reprocess the unsealed jars.

Nutritional Information (1 tbsp):

Calories: 70; Total fat: 3 oz; Total carbohydrates: 8 oz; Protein: 5 oz

# Apples & Orange Jelly

---

## *Prep Time: 1 hour | Makes: 8 10 oz jars*

---

Ingredients:

2 lb apples, diced

4 oranges, peeled and diced

5 cups of sugar

2 tsp. cinnamon


How to Prepare:

1.  Spoon 1 cup of the sugar over the apples and oranges. Set aside for overnight.

2.  Boil the apples and oranges over the low heat for around 30 minutes, stirring all the time. Pour in some water. Then mash the apples and oranges using the potato masher and strain the mixture to get 4-5 cups of the juice.

3.  In a saucepan, combine the juice with the remaining sugar and boil the juice for 30 minutes until thickened. The jelly should be thick enough to pour it into the jars. Skim the foam from the surface. 10 minutes before the jelly is ready mix in the cinnamon.

4.  Remove the saucepan from the heat and pour the freshly cooked jelly into the sterilized jars.

5.  Turn the jars upside down or boil for around 10 minutes and then leave to cool. Check the lids by pressing them with the finger. In case some of the jars with the jelly are unsealed, place them into the fridge or reprocess the unsealed jars.

Nutritional Information (1 tbsp):

Calories: 57; Total fat: 4 oz; Total carbohydrates: 8 oz; Protein: 3 oz

---

***Prep Time: 40 min. | Makes: 4-5 12 oz jars***

---

Ingredients:

4 lb peaches, washed and sliced

3 tbsp. lemon zest, minced

5 cups of sugar

4 tbsp. lemon juice

1 tbsp. pure vanilla exam

How to Prepare:

1. In a large saucepan, combine the peaches and sugar and boil over medium heat for around 40 minutes, stirring all the time with a spoon until the sugar dissolves. Take a big spoon and remove the scum from the surface. Spoon some jam on a plate and wait until thickened, if not continue boiling and testing. Add more sugar. The jam should be thick enough to spoon it into jars. Few minutes before the jam is ready, stir in the pure vanilla extract, lemon juice and lemon zest and keep stirring until the peach mixture has thickened.

2. When the jam is ready, remove the saucepan from the heat and spoon freshly cooked jam into sterilized jars up to 1/5 inch from the top.

3. Seal the jars and then place them into the boiling water. In a large pot, boil the jars for around 10 minutes and then take them out and leave to cool. Check the lids by pressing them with the finger. In case some of the jars with the lemon peach jam are unsealed, place them into the fridge or reprocess the unsealed jars.

Nutritional Information (1 tbsp):

Calories: 69; Total fat: 2 oz; Total carbohydrates: 5.6 oz; Protein: 6 oz

# Rose Petals & Raspberries Jelly

*Prep Time: 50 min.* | *Makes: 6-7 11 oz jars*

## Ingredients:

25 oz raspberries, fresh

10 oz rose petals

5 cups of sugar

3 tbsp. pure vanilla extract

## How to Prepare:

1. Spoon 4 tbsp. sugar over the raspberries. Set aside for few hours.

2. In a pan, heat the water and boil the rose petals on a low heat for about 15-20 minutes. Spoon some sugar.

3. Pour some water and boil the raspberries on a low heat for around 15-20 minutes, stirring all the time. Then strain the raspberries to get 4 cups of the juice.

4. In a saucepan, combine the juice with the sugar, rose petals and pure vanilla extract. Boil the juice for 30 minutes. The jelly should be thick enough to pour it into the jars.

5. Remove the saucepan from the heat and ladle the freshly cooked jelly into the sterilized jars and seal the jars.

6. Flip the jars upside down or boil for around 10 minutes and then leave to cool. Check the lids by pressing them with the finger. In case some of the jars with the rose petals raspberries jelly are unsealed, place them into the fridge or reprocess the unsealed jars.

## Nutritional Information (1 tbsp):

Calories: 54; Total fat: 2 oz; Total carbohydrates: 9 oz; Protein: 3 oz

# Tasty Blueberry Jam

---

*Prep Time: 30 min.* | *Makes: 5-6 10 oz jars*

---

Ingredients:

4 cups of blueberries, fresh or frozen

5 cups of sugar

4 tbsp. honey

4 tsp. lemon juice

How to Prepare:

1. Defrost the blueberries by leaving them in a bowl at room temperature for at least few hours or place the blueberries in the fridge overnight.

2. Spoon the blueberries into a blender and lightly puree them.

3. In a big saucepan, combine the blueberries, sugar, and honey and boil over medium heat for around 20 minutes, stirring all the time with a spoon until the sugar dissolves. Remove the foam and the scum from the blueberry jam.

4. 5 minutes before the jam is ready mix in the lemon juice and keep stirring until the blueberries jam has thickened. Spoon some blueberry jam on a plate and wait until thickened, if not continue boiling and testing until thickened.

5.  When the jam is ready, remove the pot with the blueberries from the heat and pour freshly cooked jam into sterilized jars up to 1/5 inch from the top.

6.  Seal the jars and then place them into the boiling water. In a large pot, boil the jars for around 10 minutes and then take them out and leave to cool. Check the lids by pressing them with the finger. In case some of the jars with the blueberry jam are unsealed, place them into the fridge or reprocess the unsealed jars.

**Nutritional Information (1 tbsp):**

Calories: 59; Total fat: 2 oz; Total carbohydrates: 4 oz; Protein: 1 oz

# Mixed Berry Jam

---

*Prep Time: 40 min.* | *Makes: 5-6 11 oz jars*

---

Ingredients:

2 cups of blueberries, fresh

1 cup of small strawberries, fresh

1 cup of raspberries, fresh

5 cups of sugar

1 tsp. citric acid or lemon juice

How to Prepare:

1. In a large saucepan, combine the berries with the sugar and leave for at least 5 hours or overnight. (unrefrigerated at room temperature)

2. Bring the berries to the boil and continue boiling over medium heat, stirring all the time until thickened and removing the foam from the surface. Few minutes before the jam is ready mix in the citric acid or lemon juice.

3. Ladle the jam into sterilized jars up to 1/5 inch from the top.

4. Seal the jars and then flip the jars upside down or boil for around 7-10 minutes and then leave to cool.

Nutritional Information (1 tbsp):

Calories: 51; Total fat: 2 oz; Total carbohydrates: 1.9 oz; Protein: 1 oz

# Cherry & Plum Jelly

---

*Prep Time: 1 hour | Makes: 6-7 11 oz jars*

---

Ingredients:

2 lbs cherries, pitted

1 lbs plums, pitted

5 cups of sugar

2 tsp. citric acid

How to Prepare:

1.  Spoon 1 cup of sugar over the berries and set aside for overnight.

2.  Pour some water and boil the berries over the low heat for around 30 minutes, stirring all the time. Then mash the berries with the potato masher and strain the mixture to get 4-5 cups of the juice.

3.  In a saucepan, combine the juice with the remaining sugar and boil the juice for 30 minutes until thickened. The jelly should be thick enough to pour it into the jars. Skim the foam from the surface. 10 minutes before the jelly is ready mix in the citric acid.

4.  Remove the saucepan from the heat and pour the freshly cooked jelly into the sterilized jars.

5.  Turn the jars upside down or boil for around 10 minutes and then leave to cool. Check the lids by pressing them with the finger. In case some of the jars with the cherry jelly are unsealed, place them into the fridge or reprocess the unsealed jars.

Nutritional Information (1 tbsp):

Calories: 65; Total fat: 5 oz; Total carbohydrates: 7 oz; Protein: 3 oz

# Pears-Alpine Strawberry Jam

*Prep Time: 40 min.* | *Makes: 3-4 10 oz jars*

Ingredients:

2-2.5 lb Alpine strawberries

4 medium pears, diced

4 cups of sugar

1 tsp. citric acid

How to Prepare:

1. Spoon the sugar over the Alpine strawberries and pears. Set aside for at least few hours.

2. Boil the Alpine strawberries with the pears and sugar over medium heat for 40 minutes, stirring all the time until thickened. Remove the scum from the surface. Few minutes before the jam is ready mix in the citric acid.

3. Pour the Alpine strawberries and pears jam into the sterilized jars up to 1/5 inch from the top.

4. Seal the jars and then flip the jars upside down or boil for around 7-10 minutes and then leave to cool. Check the lids by pressing them with the finger. In case some of

the jars with the Alpine strawberry jam are unsealed, place them into the fridge or reprocess the unsealed jars.

Nutritional Information (1 tbsp):

Calories: 70; Total fat: 2 oz; Total carbohydrates: 8 oz; Protein: 3 oz

# Raspberry Jelly

***Prep Time: 50 min. | Makes: 7-8 10 oz jars***

Ingredients:

25 oz raspberries, fresh

5 cups of sugar

1 medium lemon, halved and squeezed

3 tbsp. pure vanilla extract

How to Prepare:

1. Spoon 4 tbsp. sugar over the raspberries. Set aside for few hours. Then mash the raspberries using the potato masher.

2. Pour some water and boil the raspberries on a low heat for around 15-20 minutes, stirring all the time. Then strain the raspberries to get 4 cups of the juice.

3. In a saucepan, combine the juice with the sugar and pure vanilla extract. Pour the lemon juice. Boil the strawberry juice for 30 minutes. The jelly should be thick enough to pour it into the jars.

4. Remove the saucepan from the heat and ladle the freshly cooked jelly into the sterilized jars and seal the jars.

5. Flip the jars upside down or boil for around 10 minutes and then leave to cool. Check the lids by pressing them with the finger. In case some of the jars with the raspberry jelly are unsealed, place them into the fridge or reprocess the unsealed jars.

Nutritional Information (1 tbsp):

Calories: 52; Total fat: 3 oz; Total carbohydrates: 8 oz; Protein: 2 oz

# Vanilla Blueberry Jelly

---

*Prep Time: 1 hour | Makes: 6-7 11 oz jars*

---

Ingredients:

3 lbs blueberries

5 cups of sugar

2 tsp. citric acid

2 tsp. vanilla

How to Prepare:

1.  Spoon 1 cup of the sugar over the berries and set aside for overnight.

2.  Boil the blueberries over the low heat for around 30 minutes, stirring all the time. Pour in some water. Then mash the blueberries with the potato masher and strain the mixture to get 4-5 cups of the juice.

3.  In a saucepan, combine the juice with the remaining sugar and vanilla and boil the juice for 30 minutes until thickened. The jelly should be thick enough to pour it into the jars. Skim the foam from the surface. 10 minutes before the jelly is ready mix in the citric acid.

4.  Remove the saucepan from the heat and pour the freshly cooked jelly into the sterilized jars.

5.  Turn the jars upside down or boil for around 10 minutes and then leave to cool. Check the lids by pressing them with the finger. In case some of the jars with the jelly are unsealed, place them into the fridge or reprocess the unsealed jars.

Nutritional Information (1 tbsp):

Calories: 57; Total fat: 4 oz; Total carbohydrates: 8 oz; Protein: 3 oz

# Tangerine-Cherry Jam

*Prep Time: 30 min. | Makes: 5-6 11 oz jars*

Ingredients:

8 cups of cherries, washed and pitted

0.5 lbs tangerines

4 cups of sugar

3 tbsp. orange juice

How to Prepare:

1. Spoon the sugar over the cherries and pour few glasses of water. Spoon the tangerines and then boil the cherries over low heat for 30 minutes, stirring all the time.

2. Remove the foam from the surface.

3. Remove the saucepan from the heat and ladle the freshly cooked jam into the sterilized jars and seal them.

4. Flip the jars upside down or boil for around 10 minutes and then leave to cool. Check the lids by pressing them with the finger. In case some of the jars are unsealed, place them into the fridge or reprocess the unsealed jars.

Nutritional Information (1 tbsp):

Calories: 52; Total fat: 6 oz; Total carbohydrates: 11 oz; Protein: 4 oz

# Vanilla & Cherry Jam

---

*Prep Time: 20 min.*│*Makes: 4-5 11 oz jars*

---

Ingredients:

4 cups of cherries, washed and pitted

1 tbsp. vanilla

4 cups of sugar

1 tsp. citric acid

How to Prepare:

1. Spoon the sugar over the cherries and pour few glasses of water, and then boil the cherries over low heat for 15-20 minutes, stirring all the time.

2. Remove the foam from the surface and stir in the vanilla.

3. Remove the saucepan from the heat and ladle the freshly cooked jam into the sterilized jars and seal them.

4. Flip the jars upside down or boil for around 10 minutes and then leave to cool. Check the lids by pressing them with the finger. In case some of the jars with the cherry jam are unsealed, place them into the fridge or reprocess the unsealed jars.

Nutritional Information (1 tbsp):

Calories: 55; Total fat: 1 oz; Total carbohydrates: 3 oz; Protein: 1.5 oz

# Blueberry & Raspberry Jelly

***Prep Time: 50 min. | Makes: 8 10 oz jars***

Ingredients:

1 lbs blueberries

1 lbs raspberries

5 cups of sugar

2 tsp. citric acid

How to Prepare:

1. Spoon 1 cup of the sugar over the berries. Set aside for overnight.

2. Boil the blueberries and raspberries over the low heat for around 20 minutes, stirring all the time. Pour in some water. Then mash the blueberries and raspberries using the potato masher and strain the mixture to get 4-5 cups of the juice.

3. In a saucepan, combine the juice with the remaining sugar and boil the juice for 30 minutes until thickened. The jelly should be thick enough to pour it into the jars. Skim the foam from the surface. 10 minutes before the jelly is ready mix in the citric acid.

4. Remove the saucepan from the heat and pour the freshly cooked jelly into the sterilized jars.

5. Turn the jars upside down or boil for around 10 minutes and then leave to cool. Check the lids by pressing them with the finger. In case some of the jars with the jelly are unsealed, place them into the fridge or reprocess the unsealed jars.

Nutritional Information (1 tbsp):

Calories: 52; Total fat: 6 oz; Total carbohydrates: 9 oz; Protein: 4 oz

# Apricots Taste Redcurrant Jelly

***Prep Time: 50 min. | Makes: 6-7 11 oz jars***

## Ingredients:

6 cups of redcurrants, fresh

3 tbsp. pure apricots extract

5 cups of sugar

1 cup of orange juice

## How to Prepare:

1. Spoon 4 tbsp. sugar over the redcurrants and set aside for few hours and then crush the berries.

2. Pour some water and boil the redcurrants over the low heat for 15-20 minutes, stirring all the time. Then strain the redcurrants to get 4 cups of the juice.

3. In a saucepan, combine the juice with the sugar and boil the juice for 30 minutes. Pour the orange juice. Mix well. The jelly should be thick enough to ladle it into the jars. Remove the foam from the surface. 10 minutes before the jelly is ready mix in the pure apricots extract.

4. Remove the saucepan from the heat and ladle the freshly cooked jelly into the sterilized jars and seal the jars.

5. Flip the jars upside down or boil for around 10 minutes and then leave to cool. Check the lids by pressing them with the finger. In case some of the jars with the redcurrant jelly are unsealed, place them into the fridge or reprocess the unsealed jars.

## Nutritional Information (1 tbsp):

Calories: 56; Total fat: 3 oz; Total carbohydrates: 5 oz; Protein: 3 oz

# Redcurrant Jam

***Prep Time: 40 min. | Makes: 5-6 11 oz jars***

Ingredients:

4 cups of redcurrants, fresh

6 cups of sugar

1 tsp. vanilla

How to Prepare:

1.  Wash the redcurrants and boil the berries with the sugar over medium heat for 40 minutes, stirring all the time until thickened. Remove the foam from the surface.

2.  Spoon some jam on a plate and wait until thickened, if not continue boiling and testing. The jam should be thick enough to spoon it into jars. Few minutes before the jam is ready stir in the vanilla.

3.  When the jam is ready, remove the saucepan from the heat and ladle freshly cooked redcurrant jam into sterilized jars up to 1/5 inch from the top and seal the jars.

4.  Flip the jars with the redcurrant jam upside down or boil for around 10 minutes and then leave to cool. Check the lids by pressing them with the finger. In case some of the jars with the redcurrant jam are unsealed, place them into the fridge or reprocess the unsealed jars.

Nutritional Information (1 tbsp):

Calories: 54; Total fat: 5 oz; Total carbohydrates: 8 oz; Protein: 2 oz

# Orange Plum Jam

---

*Prep Time: 40 min. | Makes: 6-7 11 oz jars*

---

## Ingredients:

5 lb plums, pitted and halved

2 oranges, cubed

1 tbsp. orange zest, minced

4 cups of sugar

2 tbsp. orange juice

1 tsp. cinnamon

## How to Prepare:

1. Boil the plums and oranges with the sugar over medium heat for around 40 minutes, stirring all the time until thickened. Remove the foam from the surface.

2. Spoon some jam on a plate and wait until thickened, if not continue boiling and testing. The jam should be thick enough to spoon it into the jars. Few minutes before the jam is ready stir in the orange zest, orange juice, and cinnamon.

3. When the jam is ready, remove the saucepan from the heat and ladle freshly cooked plum jam into sterilized jars up to 1/5 inch from the top and seal the jars.

4. Flip the jars with the plum jam upside down or boil for around 10 minutes and then leave to cool.


Nutritional Information (1 tbsp):

Calories: 59; Total fat: 10 oz; Total carbohydrates: 8 oz; Protein: 2 oz

# Baked Apple Jam

---

*Prep Time: 50 min.│Makes: 6-7 11 oz jars*

---

Ingredients:

5 lb sweet Gala or Fuji apples, peeled and cubed

4 cups of sugar

2 tbsp. citric acid

1 tbsp. cinnamon

How to Prepare:

1. Preheat the oven to 300°-350° Fahrenheit, combine the apples with the sugar and mix in the citric acid and cinnamon to bake the apples for around 50 minutes until thickened, if not continue baking.

2. Spoon the freshly baked jam into the sterilized jars up to 1/5 inch from the top and seal the jars.

3. Flip the jars upside down or boil for around 10 minutes and then leave to cool.

Nutritional Information (1 tbsp):

Calories: 59; Total fat: 4 oz; Total carbohydrates: 10 oz; Protein: 3 oz

# Vanilla Raspberry Jelly

*Prep Time: 1 hour | Makes: 8 10 oz jars*

Ingredients:

3 lbs raspberries

5 cups of sugar

2 tsp. citric acid

3 tsp. pure vanilla extract

How to Prepare:

1. Spoon 1 cup of the sugar over the berries. Set aside for overnight.

2. Boil the raspberries over the low heat for around 30 minutes, stirring all the time. Pour in some water. Then mash the berries using the potato masher and strain the mixture to get 4-5 cups of the juice.

3. In a saucepan, combine the juice with the remaining sugar and boil the juice for 30 minutes until thickened. The jelly should be thick enough to pour it into the jars. Skim the foam from the surface. 10 minutes before the jelly is ready mix in the citric acid and pure vanilla extract.

4. Remove the saucepan from the heat and pour the freshly cooked jelly into the sterilized jars.

5. Turn the jars upside down or boil for around 10 minutes and then leave to cool. Check the lids by pressing them with the finger. In case some of the jars with the jelly are unsealed, place them into the fridge or reprocess the unsealed jars.

Nutritional Information (1 tbsp):

Calories: 58; Total fat: 6 oz; Total carbohydrates: 10 oz; Protein: 4 oz

# Pineapple & Apple Jam

---

*Prep Time: 40 min. | Makes: 4-5 10 oz jars*

---

Ingredients:

2 medium pineapples, peeled and diced

2 lbs big apples, peeled and sliced

4 cups of sugar

1 cup of water

1 tsp. Cinnamon

1 tsp. citric acid

How to Prepare:

1.  Spoon the sugar over the fruits and set aside for few hours. Boil the pineapples and the apples with the sugar and the water over medium heat for around 40 minutes, stirring all the time until the sugar dissolves. Remove the foam from the surface.

2.  The jam should be thick enough to spoon it into the jars. Few minutes before the jam is ready mix in the cinnamon and citric acid.

3.  When the jam is ready, remove the saucepan from the heat and ladle freshly cooked jam into sterilized jars up to 1/5 inch from the top.

4. Seal the jars and then process them in a water bath. In a large pot, boil the jars for around 10 minutes and then take them out and leave to cool. Check the lids by pressing them with the finger. In case some of the jars are unsealed, place them into the fridge or reprocess the unsealed jars.

Nutritional Information (1 tbsp):

Calories: 53; Total fat: 7 oz; Total carbohydrates: 10 oz; Protein: 4 oz

# Blackcurrants & Apples Jam

---

*Prep Time: 30 min.│Makes: 4-5 11 oz jars*

---

## Ingredients:

3 lb blackcurrants

4 big apples, peeled and sliced

5 cups of sugar

1 tsp. Cinnamon

1 tsp. lemon juice

## How to Prepare:

1. Spoon the sugar over the fruits and set aside for few hours. Boil the blackcurrants and the apples with the sugar and some water over medium heat for around 30 minutes, stirring all the time until the sugar dissolves. Remove the foam from the surface.

2. The jam should be thick enough to spoon it into the jars. Few minutes before the jam is ready mix in the cinnamon and lemon juice.

3. When the jam is ready, remove the saucepan from the heat and ladle freshly cooked jam into sterilized jars up to 1/5 inch from the top.

4. Flip the jars upside down or boil for around 15 minutes and then leave to cool.

## Nutritional Information (1 tbsp):

Calories: 53; Total fat: 8 oz; Total carbohydrates: 10 oz; Protein: 3 oz

# Vanilla & Pears Jam

***Prep Time: 30 min.*** | ***Makes: 4-5 11 oz jars***

Ingredients:

5 big pears, peeled and cubed

4 cups of sugar

½ cup of water

1 tsp. vanilla

1 tsp. citric acid

How to Prepare:

1. Boil the pears with the sugar, vanilla, citric acid and some water over medium heat for around 30 minutes, stirring all the time until the sugar dissolves. Remove the foam from the surface.

2. Spoon the freshly cooked jam into sterilized jars up to 1/5 inch from the top.

3. Seal the jars and then process them in a water bath. In a large pot, boil the jars for around 10 minutes and then take them out and leave to cool. Check the lids by pressing them with the finger. In case some of the jars with the vanilla and pear jam are unsealed, place them into the fridge or reprocess the unsealed jars.

Nutritional Information (1 tbsp):

Calories: 53; Total fat: 3 oz; Total carbohydrates: 8 oz; Protein: 2 oz

# Orange-Pears Jam

*Prep Time: 30 min.* | *Makes: 4-5 11 oz jars*

Ingredients:

5 big pears, peeled and cubed

4 cups of sugar

2 tbsp. orange zest, minced

½ cup of orange juice

1 tsp. vanilla

How to Prepare:

1. Boil the pears with the sugar, vanilla, orange zest and orange juice over medium heat for around 30 minutes, stirring all the time until the sugar dissolves. Remove the foam from the surface.

2. Spoon the freshly cooked jam into sterilized jars up to 1/5 inch from the top.

3. Seal the jars and then process them in a water bath. In a large pot, boil the jars for around 10 minutes and then take them out and leave to cool. Check the lids by pressing them with the finger. In case some of the jars with the orange and pear jam are unsealed, place them into the fridge or reprocess the unsealed jars.

Nutritional Information (1 tbsp):

Calories: 52; Total fat: 3 oz; Total carbohydrates: 7 oz; Protein: 2 oz

# Pineapple Taste Cherry Jelly

*Prep Time: 1 hour | Makes: 6-7 11 oz jars*

Ingredients:

2 lbs cherries, pitted

2 tbsp. pure pineapple extract

5 cups of sugar

2 tsp. citric acid

How to Prepare:

1. Spoon 1 cup of sugar over the berries and set aside for overnight.

2. Boil the berries over the low heat for around 30 minutes, stirring all the time. Then add in the pure pineapple extract and mash the berries with the potato masher. Strain the mixture to get 5 cups of the juice.

3. In a saucepan, combine the juice with the remaining sugar and boil the juice for around 30 minutes until thickened. The jelly should be thick enough to pour it into the jars. Skim the foam from the surface. 10 minutes before the jelly is ready mix in the citric acid.

4. Remove the saucepan from the heat and pour the freshly cooked jelly into the sterilized jars.

5. Turn the jars upside down or boil for around 10 minutes and then leave to cool. Check the lids by pressing them with the finger. In case some of the jars with the cherry jelly are unsealed, place them into the fridge or reprocess the unsealed jars.

Nutritional Information (1 tbsp):

Calories: 57; Total fat: 4 oz; Total carbohydrates: 8 oz; Protein: 3 oz

# Sugar-Free Apricot Jam

---

*Prep Time: 40 min. | Makes around 5 10 oz jars*

---

Ingredients:

3 lb apricots, cubed

3 tbsp. erythritol

20 drops of stevia

4 tbsp. honey

2 tsp. citric acid


How to Prepare:

1. Wash and cube the apricots and place them into a big saucepan and then spoon the honey over the apricots. Crack few apricot stones and place the apricot kernels into the saucepan, this step will add specific flavors and an unforgettable taste to your apricot jam.

2. Boil the apricots over medium heat for around 40 minutes, stirring all the time. Remember to remove the foam from the surface.

3. Mix in the erythritol, stevia and citric acid and keep stirring until the apricots mixture has gelled. Put some jam on the plate and press down with your finger to check the density. Continue boiling and testing every five minutes until thickened.

4. Remove the saucepan with the sugar-free apricot jam from the heat and carefully pour freshly cooked jam into the hot and sterilized jars up to 1/4 inch from the top.

5. Seal the jars and then turn them upside down or boil for around 10 minutes and then leave to cool. Check the lids by pressing them with the finger. In case some of the jars with the apricot jam are unsealed, place them into the fridge or reprocess the unsealed jars.

Nutritional Information (1 tbsp):

Calories: 48; Total fat: 2 oz; Total carbohydrates: 4 oz; Protein: 1 oz

# Apple Pumpkin Jam

---

*Prep Time: 50 min. | Makes around 8 11 oz jars*

---

Ingredients:

3 lb pumpkin, peeled and cubed

2 apples, peeled and sliced

4 cups of sugar

half cup of apple juice

How to Prepare:

1. Place the pumpkin and apples into a big saucepan and spoon the sugar on top and leave for at least few hours unrefrigerated at room temperature or place in the fridge overnight.

2. In a saucepan, combine the pumpkin, apples, and apple juice and simmer the pumpkin mixture for 40 minutes until the sugar dissolves and pumpkin is soft. Remember to skim the foam from the surface. The apple pumpkin jam should be gelled enough to ladle it into the jars.

3. Ladle the freshly cooked apple pumpkin jam into the sterilized and hot jars and seal the jars.

4. Flip the jars upside down or boil for around 10 minutes and then leave to cool. In case some of the jars with the apple pumpkin jam are unsealed, place them into the fridge or reprocess the unsealed jars.

Nutritional Information (1 tbsp):
Calories: 55; Total fat: 0 oz; Total carbohydrates: 0.8 oz; Protein: 0 oz

# Orange Gooseberry Jam

---

*Prep Time: 40 min.* | *Makes around 6 11 oz jars*

---

Ingredients:

5 lb gooseberries

2 oranges, sliced

2 tbsp. orange zest, minced

5 cups of sugar

3 tbsp. orange juice

How to Prepare:

1. In a saucepan, combine the gooseberries and oranges with the sugar and leave for few hours unrefrigerated at room temperature. Then boil the gooseberries and oranges with the sugar for 40 minutes, stirring until the sugar dissolves. Skim the foam and scum from the surface.

2. Five minutes before the jam is ready mix in the orange juice and orange zest and keep stirring until the orange gooseberry jam has gelled.

3. Ladle freshly cooked orange gooseberry jam into hot and sterilized jars up to 1/5 inch from the top and then seal the jars.

4. Flip the jars with the orange gooseberry jam upside down or boil for around 10 minutes and then leave to cool. Check the lids by pressing them with the finger. In case some of the jars with the orange gooseberry jam are unsealed, place them into the fridge or reprocess the unsealed jars.

Nutritional Information (1 tbsp):

Calories: 48; Total fat: 0 oz; Total carbohydrates: 1 oz; Protein: 0 oz

# Cherry Peach Jam

## *Prep Time: 40 min.│ Makes around 6 11 oz jars*

Ingredients:

4 cups cherries, washed and stoned

2 lb peaches, washed and sliced

5 cups of sugar

2 tbsp. lemon juice or 2 tsp. citric acid

How to Prepare:

1. In a big pot, combine the sliced peaches with the cherries and add the sugar on top. Leave for few hours unrefrigerated at room temperature.

2. Boil the fruits with the sugar for 40 minutes, stirring until the sugar dissolves. Remove the foam from the jam surface.

3. Few minutes before the jam is ready mix in the lemon juice or citric acid and keep stirring until the jam has gelled.

4. Spoon the freshly cooked cherry peach jam into the sterilized jars up to 1/5 inch from the top and then seal the jars.

5. Now turn the jars upside down and leave them for at least ten hours or for overnight to cool completely and only then turn them back. Check the lids by pressing them with the finger. In case some of the jars with the cherry peach jam are unsealed, place them into the fridge or reprocess the unsealed jars.

Nutritional Information (1 tbsp):
Calories: 67; Total fat: 0.4 oz; Total carbohydrates: 2 oz; Protein: 1 oz

# Lemon Apricot Jam

---

*Prep Time: 40 min.* | *Makes around 6 11 oz jars*

---

Ingredients:

4 lb apricots, washed and sliced

3 tbsp. lemon zest, minced

5 cups of sugar

4 tbsp. lemon juice

How to Prepare:

1. In a large saucepan, combine the apricots and sugar and boil over medium heat for around 40 minutes, stirring all the time with a spoon until the sugar dissolves. Take a big spoon and remove the scum from the surface.

2. Spoon some jam on a plate and wait until gelled, if not continue boiling and testing. The jam should be thick enough to spoon it into the jars.

3. Few minutes before the jam is ready mix in the lemon juice and lemon zest and keep stirring until the apricot mixture has thickened.

4. When the lemon apricot jam is ready, remove the saucepan from the heat and spoon freshly cooked jam into sterilized jars up to 1/5 inch from the top.

5. Seal the jars with the lemon apricot jam and flip them upside down or boil for around 10 minutes and then leave to cool. Check the lids by pressing them with the finger. In case some of the jars with the lemon apricot jam are unsealed, place them into the fridge or reprocess the unsealed jars.

Nutritional Information (1 tbsp):

Calories: 64; Total fat: 0.2 oz; Total carbohydrates: 1.6 oz; Protein: 0 oz

# Vanilla Blueberry Jam

---

*Prep Time: 40 min. | Makes around 6 10 oz jars*

---

Ingredients:

5 cups of blueberries, fresh

5 cups of sugar

3 tsp. vanilla

How to Prepare:

1. In a big pot, combine the blueberries, sugar, and vanilla and boil over medium heat for around 40 minutes, stirring all the time until the sugar dissolves. Remove the foam and the scum from the vanilla blueberry jam.

2. Spoon some vanilla blueberry jam on a plate and wait until gelled. Check by pressing with the finger or the spoon, if not gelled enough continue boiling and testing every 5-10 minutes until gelled.

3. When the vanilla blueberry jam is ready, remove the pot with the blueberries from the heat and pour freshly cooked jam into sterilized and hot jars up to 1/4 inch from the top.

4. Seal the jars with the vanilla blueberry jam and flip them upside down or boil them for around 10 minutes and then leave to cool. Check the lids by pressing them with the finger. In case some of the jars with the vanilla blueberry jam are unsealed, place them into the fridge or reprocess the unsealed jars.

Nutritional Information (1 tbsp):
Calories: 59; Total fat: 3 oz; Total carbohydrates: 4 oz; Protein: 2 oz

# Blueberry Pears Jelly

---

## *Prep Time: 1 hour | Makes: 8 10 oz jars*

---

Ingredients:

3 lb blueberries

1 lb pears, peeled and diced

5 cups of sugar

2 tsp. citric acid

How to Prepare:

1. Spoon 1 cup of the sugar over the berries and pears. Set aside for overnight.

2. Boil the blueberries and pears over the low heat for around 30 minutes, stirring all the time. Pour in some water. Then mash the blueberries and pears using the potato masher and strain the mixture to get 4-5 cups of the juice.

3. In a saucepan, combine the juice with the remaining sugar and boil the juice for 30 minutes until thickened. The jelly should be thick enough to pour it into the jars. Skim the foam from the surface. 10 minutes before the jelly is ready mix in the citric acid.

4. Remove the saucepan from the heat and pour the freshly cooked jelly into the sterilized jars.

5. Turn the jars upside down or boil for around 10 minutes and then leave to cool. Check the lids by pressing them with the finger. In case some of the jars with the jelly are unsealed, place them into the fridge or reprocess the unsealed jars.

Nutritional Information (1 tbsp):

Calories: 57; Total fat: 4 oz; Total carbohydrates: 8 oz; Protein: 3 oz

# Mango-Raspberry Jam

*Prep Time: 50 min.* | *Makes: 3-4 10 oz jars*

**Ingredients:**

2 lb raspberries

3 medium mangos, peeled and diced

4 cups of sugar

5 tbsp. orange juice

**How to Prepare:**

1. Spoon the sugar over the raspberries and set aside for at least few hours.

2. Boil the raspberries with the sugar on a medium heat for 40 minutes, stirring all the time until thickened. Remove the scum from the surface. Few minutes before the jam is ready mix in the orange juice.

3. Pour the raspberry jam into the sterilized jars up to 1/4 inch from the top and seal the jars. Then flip the jars upside down or boil for around 10 minutes and then leave to cool. Check the lids by pressing them with the finger. In case some of the jars with the jam are unsealed, place them into the fridge or reprocess the unsealed jars.

**Nutritional Information (1 tbsp):**

Calories: 57; Total fat: 5 oz; Total carbohydrates: 9 oz; Protein: 4 oz

# Blackberry Jelly

*Prep Time: 1 hour | Makes: 8 10 oz jars*

Ingredients:

3 lb blackberries

5 cups of sugar

3 tsp. citric acid

How to Prepare:

1. Spoon 1 cup of the sugar over the berries. Set aside for overnight.

2. Boil the blackberries on a low heat for around 30 minutes, stirring all the time. Pour in some water. Then mash the blackberries using the potato masher and strain the mixture to get 4-5 cups of the juice.

3. In a saucepan, combine the juice with the remaining sugar and boil the juice for 30 minutes until thickened. The jelly should be thick enough to pour it into the jars. Skim the foam from the surface. 10 minutes before the jelly is ready mix in the citric acid.

4. Remove the saucepan from the heat and pour the freshly cooked jelly into the sterilized jars or bottles.

5. Turn the jars upside down or boil for around 10 minutes and then leave to cool. Check the lids by pressing them with the finger. In case some of the jars or bottles with the blackberry jelly are unsealed, place them into the fridge or reprocess the unsealed jars.

Nutritional Information (1 tbsp):

Calories: 58; Total fat: 6 oz; Total carbohydrates: 10 oz; Protein: 4 oz

# Blackberry & Strawberry Jelly

---

*Prep Time: 1 hour | Makes: 7 12 oz jars*

---

Ingredients:

3 lb blackberries

2 lb strawberries

5 cups of sugar

3 tsp. citric acid

How to Prepare:

1. Spoon 1 cup of the sugar over the berries. Set aside for overnight.

2. Boil the blackberries and strawberries on a low heat for around 30 minutes, stirring all the time. Pour in some water. Then mash the berries using the potato masher and strain the mixture to get 5-6 cups of juice.

3. In a saucepan, combine the juice with the remaining sugar and boil the juice for 30 minutes until thickened. The jelly should be thick enough to pour it into the jars. Skim the foam from the surface. 10 minutes before the jelly is ready mix in the citric acid.

4. Remove the saucepan from the heat and pour the freshly cooked jelly into the sterilized jars or bottles.

5. Turn the jars upside down or boil for around 10 minutes and then leave to cool. Check the lids by pressing them with the finger. In case some of the jars or bottles with the jelly are unsealed, place them into the fridge or reprocess the unsealed jars.

Nutritional Information (1 tbsp):

Calories: 67; Total fat: 8 oz; Total carbohydrates: 14 oz; Protein: 5 oz

# Fig-Apple Jam

***Prep Time: 40 min. | Makes around 6-7 10 oz jars***

Ingredients:

30 oz figs, diced

10 sour apples

5 cups of sugar

3 tsp. vanilla

2 tsp. citric acid

How to Prepare:

1. Wash and peel the apples and then cube them. Spoon the sugar and citric acid over the apples and set aside for around 1 to 2 hours unrefrigerated at room temperature or place in the fridge for few hours.

2. Boil the apples and figs with the sugar over medium heat for around 40 minutes, stirring all the time.

3. Few minutes before the apple jam is ready mix in the vanilla. Remove the saucepan from the heat and ladle freshly cooked jam into sterilized jars up to 1/5 inch from the top.

4. Flip the jars with the fig apple jam upside down or boil for around 10 minutes and then leave to cool. Check the lids by pressing them with the finger. In case some of the jars with the jam are unsealed, place them into the fridge or reprocess the unsealed jars.

Nutritional Information (1 tbsp):

Calories: 52; Total fat: 4 oz; Total carbohydrates: 12 oz; Protein: 5 oz

# Blackberry & Orange Jelly

---

*Prep Time: 1 hour | Makes: 7 12 oz jars*

---

**Ingredients:**

3 lb blackberries

2 lb oranges, peeled and squeezed

2 tbsp. agar-agar

5 cups of sugar

**How to Prepare:**

1. Spoon 1 cup of the sugar over the blackberries. Set aside for overnight.

2. Boil the blackberries on a low heat for around 30 minutes, stirring all the time. Pour in some water. Then mash the berries using the potato masher and strain the mixture to get 5-6 cups of juice. Peel and squeeze the oranges.

3. In a saucepan, combine the orange juice with the blackberry juice and remaining sugar. Boil the juice for 30 minutes until thickened. The jelly should be thick enough to pour it into the jars. Skim the foam from the surface. 10 minutes before the jelly is ready mix in the agar-agar.

4. Remove the saucepan from the heat and pour the freshly cooked jelly into the sterilized jars or bottles.

5. Turn the jars upside down or boil for around 10 minutes and then leave to cool. Check the lids by pressing them with the finger. In case some of the jars or bottles with the jelly are unsealed, place them into the fridge or reprocess the unsealed jars.

**Nutritional Information (1 tbsp):**

Calories: 67; Total fat: 8 oz; Total carbohydrates: 12 oz; Protein: 6 oz

# Plum Jelly with Pineapples

*Prep Time: 1 hour | Makes: 8 10 oz jars*

Ingredients:

2 lbs plums, pitted

2 lbs pineapples, diced

5 cups of sugar

2 tsp. citric acid

How to Prepare:

1. Spoon 1 cup of the sugar over the plums and pineapples. Set aside for overnight.

2. Boil the plums over the low heat for around 30 minutes, stirring all the time. Pour in some water and add the pineapples. Then mash the plums using the potato masher and strain the mixture to get 4-5 cups of juice.

3. In a saucepan, combine the juice with the remaining sugar and boil the juice for 30 minutes until thickened. The jelly should be thick enough to pour it into the jars. Skim the foam from the surface. 10 minutes before the jelly is ready mix in the citric acid.

4. Remove the saucepan from the heat and pour the freshly cooked jelly into the sterilized jars.

5. Turn the jars upside down or boil for around 10 minutes and then leave to cool. Check the lids by pressing them with the finger. In case some of the jars with the jelly are unsealed, place them into the fridge or reprocess the unsealed jars.

Nutritional Information (1 tbsp):

Calories: 59; Total fat: 5 oz; Total carbohydrates: 9 oz; Protein: 4 oz

# Blueberry-Pineapple Jam

---

*Prep Time: 40 min.* | *Makes around 6 10 oz jars*

---

Ingredients:

5 cups of blueberries, fresh

1 big pineapple, peeled and diced

5 cups of sugar

3 tsp. vanilla

How to Prepare:

1. In a big pot, combine the blueberries, pineapple cubes, sugar, and vanilla and boil over medium heat for around 40 minutes, stirring all the time until the sugar dissolves. Remove the foam and the scum from the blueberry jam.

2. Spoon some blueberry-pineapple jam on a plate and wait until gelled. Check by pressing with the finger or the spoon, if not gelled enough continue boiling and testing every 5-10 minutes until gelled.

3. When the blueberry-pineapple jam is ready, remove the pot with the blueberries from the heat and pour the freshly cooked jam into the sterilized and hot jars up to 1/4 inch from the top.

4. Seal the jars with the blueberry jam and flip them upside down or boil them for around 10 minutes and then leave to cool. Check the lids by pressing them with the finger. In case some of the jars with the blueberry jam are unsealed, place them into the fridge or reprocess the unsealed jars.

Nutritional Information (1 tbsp):
Calories: 59; Total fat: 3 oz; Total carbohydrates: 4 oz; Protein: 2 oz

# Pomegranate Jelly with Pineapples

---

### *Prep Time: 50 min. | Makes: 10-11 12 oz jars*

---

## Ingredients:

45 oz pomegranate juice

25 oz pineapple juice

2 tbsp. gelatin or agar-agar substitute

5 cups of sugar

2 tsp. citric acid

## How to Prepare:

1. Boil the pomegranate and pineapple juice over the low heat for around 20 minutes, stirring all the time. Spoon the sugar and gelatin. Boil the juice for 30 minutes until thickened. The jelly should be thick enough to pour it into the jars. Skim the foam from the surface. 10 minutes before the jelly is ready mix in the citric acid.

2. Remove the saucepan from the heat and pour the freshly cooked jelly into the sterilized jars.

3. Turn the jars upside down or boil for around 10 minutes and then leave to cool. Check the lids by pressing them with the finger. In case some of the jars with the jelly are unsealed, place them into the fridge or reprocess the unsealed jars.

## Nutritional Information (1 tbsp):

Calories: 58; Total fat: 6 oz; Total carbohydrates: 10 oz; Protein: 5 oz

# Orange Jelly with Raspberries

---

### *Prep Time: 50 min. | Makes: 6 12 oz jars*

---

## Ingredients:

2 lb oranges

1 cup of raspberry syrup

2 tbsp. gelatin or agar-agar substitute

2 cups of sugar

2 tsp. citric acid

## How to Prepare:

1. Squeeze the oranges. Then boil the orange juice with the raspberry syrup over the low heat for around 20 minutes, stirring all the time. Spoon the sugar and gelatin or its substitute. Boil the juice for 30 minutes until thickened. The jelly should be thick enough to pour it into the jars. Skim the foam from the surface. 10 minutes before the jelly is ready mix in the citric acid.

2. Remove the saucepan from the heat and pour the freshly cooked jelly into the sterilized jars.

3. Turn the jars upside down or boil for around 10 minutes and then leave to cool. Check the lids by pressing them with the finger. In case some of the jars with the orange jelly are unsealed, place them into the fridge or reprocess the unsealed jars.

## Nutritional Information (1 tbsp):

Calories: 53; Total fat: 6 oz; Total carbohydrates: 10 oz; Protein: 4 oz

# Tangerine Jelly

*Prep Time: 50 min.│Makes: 7 10 oz jars*

Ingredients:

20 oz tangerines

1 cup of strawberry syrup

2 tbsp. gelatin or agar-agar substitute

2 cups of sugar

How to Prepare:

1. Boil the tangerines with the strawberry syrup over the low heat for around 20 minutes, stirring all the time. Spoon the sugar and gelatin. Boil the juice for 30 minutes until thickened. The jelly should be thick enough to pour it into the jars. Skim the foam from the surface.

2. Remove the saucepan from the heat and pour the freshly cooked jelly into the sterilized jars.

3. Turn the jars upside down or boil for around 10 minutes and then leave to cool. Check the lids by pressing them with the finger. In case some of the jars with the jelly are unsealed, place them into the fridge or reprocess the unsealed jars.

Nutritional Information (1 tbsp):
Calories: 50; Total fat: 7 oz; Total carbohydrates: 11 oz; Protein: 6 oz

# Fig Jam with Vanilla

---

*Prep Time: 40 min. | Makes around 10 10 oz jars*

---

Ingredients:

2 lb figs, diced

1 cups of brown sugar

2 tsp. pure vanilla extract

How to Prepare:

1. Place the diced figs into a big saucepan and spoon the sugar on top. Leave for at least few hours unrefrigerated at room temperature or place in the fridge overnight.

2. Then boil the figs over the medium heat for around 10 minutes, stirring all the time until the sugar dissolves. Remove the foam from the surface. Then reduce the heat and continue to boil for around 30 minutes.

3. Mix in the pure vanilla extract and keep stirring until the figs mixture has gelled and thickened. Pour some jam on a plate and check if gelled, pressing it with the finger, if not continue boiling and testing.

4. Remove the saucepan with the fig jam from the heat and pour the freshly cooked jam into the sterilized and hot jars up to 1/5 inch from the top.

5. Seal the jars and then turn them upside down. Leave the jars for overnight to cool completely and only then turn them back.

6. Or you can do it by processing the jars in the water bath and boiling them for around 10 minutes and then leaving to cool. It is important to remember to check the lids by pressing them with the finger. In case some of the jars with the fig jam are unsealed, place them into the fridge or reprocess the unsealed jars.

Nutritional Information (1 tbsp):

Calories: 76; Total fat: 11 oz; Total carbohydrates: 12 oz; Protein: 8 oz

# Pomegranate-Cherry Jam

*Prep Time: 20 min.* | *Makes: 4-5 11 oz jars*

Ingredients:

4 cups of cherries, washed and pitted

1 cup of pomegranate juice or syrup

1 tbsp. vanilla

4 cups of sugar

1 tsp. citric acid

How to Prepare:

1. Spoon the sugar over the cherries and pour few glasses of water, and then boil the cherries over low heat for 15-20 minutes, stirring all the time.

2. Pour the pomegranate juice. Remove the foam from the surface and stir in the vanilla.

3. Remove the saucepan from the heat and ladle the freshly cooked jam into the sterilized jars and seal them.

4. Flip the jars upside down or boil for around 10 minutes and then leave to cool. Check the lids by pressing them with the finger. In case some of the jars with the cherry jam are unsealed, place them into the fridge or reprocess the unsealed jars.

Nutritional Information (1 tbsp):

Calories: 54; Total fat: 2 oz; Total carbohydrates: 4 oz; Protein: 2 oz

# Pineapple Jelly with Blackberries

*Prep Time: 50 min.* | *Makes: 5-6 8 oz jars*

**Ingredients:**

25 oz pineapple juice

1 cup of blackberry syrup

2 tbsp. gelatin or agar-agar substitute

2 cups of sugar

**How to Prepare:**

1. Boil the pineapple juice with the blackberry syrup over the low heat for around 20 minutes, stirring all the time. Spoon the sugar and gelatin. Boil the juice for 30 minutes until thickened. The jelly should be thick enough to pour it into the jars. Skim the foam from the surface.

2. Remove the saucepan from the heat and pour the freshly cooked jelly into the sterilized jars.

3. Turn the jars upside down or boil for around 10 minutes and then leave to cool. Check the lids by pressing them with the finger. In case some of the jars with the jelly are unsealed, place them into the fridge or reprocess the unsealed jars.

**Nutritional Information (1 tbsp):**

Calories: 55; Total fat: 8 oz; Total carbohydrates: 9 oz; Protein: 4 oz

# Kiwi Jam

---

### *Prep Time: 40 min.* | *Makes around 7-8 12 oz jars*

---

Ingredients:

3 lb kiwis, peeled and diced

1 tbsp. gelatin

5 cups of sugar

3 tsp. vanilla

How to Prepare:

1. In a big pot, combine the kiwis, sugar, gelatin and vanilla and boil over medium heat for around 40 minutes, stirring all the time until the sugar dissolves. Remove the foam and the scum from the jam.

2. Spoon some jam on a plate and wait until gelled. Check by pressing with the finger or the spoon, if not gelled enough continue boiling and testing every 5-10 minutes until gelled.

3. When the jam is ready, remove the pot with the fruits from the heat and pour the freshly cooked jam into the sterilized and hot jars up to 1/4 inch from the top.

4. Seal the jars and flip them upside down or boil them for around 10 minutes and then leave to cool. Check the lids by pressing them with the finger. In case some of the jars with the kiwi jam are unsealed, place them into the fridge or reprocess the unsealed jars.

Nutritional Information (1 tbsp):
Calories: 70; Total fat: 8 oz; Total carbohydrates: 13 oz; Protein: 5 oz

# Pears Jam

*__Prep Time: 45 min.__ | __Makes around 6-7 10 oz jars__*

Ingredients:

4 lb pears, diced

5 cups of sugar

3 tsp. vanilla

How to Prepare:

1. In a big pot, combine the pear cubes, sugar, and vanilla and boil over medium heat for around 40-45 minutes, stirring all the time until the sugar dissolves.

2. Spoon some jam on a plate and wait until gelled. Check by pressing with the finger or the spoon, if not gelled enough continue boiling and testing every 5-10 minutes until gelled.

3. When the jam is ready, remove the pot with the pears from the heat and pour the freshly cooked jam into the sterilized and hot jars up to 1/4 inch from the top.

4. Seal the jars and flip them upside down or boil them for around 10 minutes and then leave to cool. Check the lids by pressing them with the finger. In case some of the jars with the jam are unsealed, place them into the fridge or reprocess the unsealed jars.

Nutritional Information (1 tbsp):
Calories: 70; Total fat: 8 oz; Total carbohydrates: 11 oz; Protein: 5 oz

# Homemade Strawberry Jam

***Prep Time: 40 min.*** | ***Makes around 6 11 oz jars***

Ingredients:

8 cups of strawberries

6 cups of sugar

2 tbsp. lemon juice, freshly squeezed

1 tsp. vanilla

How to Prepare:

1. Wash and then mash the strawberries with a potato masher, blender or food processor and then spoon the sugar over the crushed strawberries.

2. Boil the berries over medium heat for around 40 minutes, stirring all the time until the sugar dissolves and don't forget to skim the foam from the strawberry jam. Add half cup of water and continue stirring.

3. 7-10 minutes before the strawberry jam is ready mix in the lemon juice and keep stirring until the strawberries mixture has thickened. Spoon some jam on a plate and wait until gelled, if not continue boiling and testing.When the jam is ready,

remove the saucepan with the strawberries from the heat and spoon freshly cooked jam into sterilized jars up to 1/5 inch from the top.

4. Seal the jars and then turn them upside down. Leave the jars for overnight to cool completely and only then turn them back. Check the lids by pressing them with the finger. In case some of the jars are unsealed, place them into the fridge or reprocess the unsealed jars.

Nutritional Information (1 tbsp):

Calories: 68; Total fat: 0.1 oz; Total carbohydrates: 1 oz; Protein: 1 oz

# Hazelnuts Gooseberry Jam

*Prep Time: 50 min.* | *Makes: 7-8 10 oz jars*

## Ingredients:

2 lb gooseberries

1 cup of hazelnuts

4 cups of brown sugar

3 tbsp. lemon juice, squeezed

2 tsp. vanilla

## How to Prepare:

1. Grind the hazelnuts. In a bowl, combine the sugar with the vanilla and mix well. Then place the gooseberries into a big saucepan and spoon the sugar-vanilla mixture on top. Leave for at least 6 hours unrefrigerated at room temperature or place in the fridge overnight.

2. In the same saucepan boil the gooseberries and sugar-vanilla mixture over high heat for around 10 minutes, stirring all the time with a spoon until sugar dissolves.

3. Then reduce the heat and continue to boil for around 40 minutes but don't forget to skim the foam from the berries.

4. Pour the lemon juice and add the nuts. Keep stirring until the berries mixture has gelled and thickened. Remove the saucepan with the gooseberries from the heat and pour the freshly cooked jam into the sterilized jars up to 1/5 inch from the top.

5. Seal the jars and then turn the jars upside down. Leave them for overnight to cool completely and only then turn them back.

## Nutritional Information (1 tbsp):

Calories: 62; Total fat: 3 oz; Total carbohydrates: 8 oz; Protein: 2 oz

# Vanilla Strawberry Jam

*Prep Time: 50 min.* | *Makes: 7-8 10 oz jars*

Ingredients:

5 lb fresh strawberries

6 cups of sugar

2 tsp. cinnamon

How to Prepare:

1. Place the strawberries into a big saucepan and spoon the sugar on top. Then sprinkle the cinnamon and leave for at least 6 hours unrefrigerated at room temperature or place in the fridge overnight.

2. In the same saucepan boil the strawberries and sugar-vanilla mixture over high heat for around 10 minutes, stirring all the time with a spoon until sugar dissolves.

3. Then reduce the heat and continue to boil for around 40 minutes but don't forget to skim the foam from the strawberries.

4. Pour the lemon juice and keep stirring until the strawberries mixture has gelled and thickened.

5. Remove the saucepan with the strawberries from the heat and pour freshly cooked jam into sterilized jars up to 1/5 inch from the top.

6. Seal the jars and then turn the jars upside down. Leave them for overnight to cool completely and only then turn them back.

7. Or you can do it more traditionally by placing the jars into the water bath and boiling for around 7-10 minutes and then leaving to cool. Check the lids by pressing them with the finger. In case some of the jars with the vanilla and strawberry jam are unsealed, place them into the fridge or reprocess the unsealed jars.

Nutritional Information (1 tbsp):

Calories: 69; Total fat: 2 oz; Total carbohydrates: 3 oz; Protein: 0.7 oz

# Orange-Blackberry Jam

---

*Prep Time: 40 min.* | *Makes: 5-6 11 oz jars*

---

## Ingredients:

3 lb fresh and sweet blackberries

2 tbsp. orange zest, minced

5 cups of sugar

1 cup of orange juice, freshly squeezed

## How to Prepare:

1. Spoon the blackberries into a food processor or blender and lightly puree them to have halves of the berries.
2. In a large saucepan, combine the berries and sugar and boil over medium heat for around 40 minutes, stirring all the time with a spoon until the sugar dissolves. Take a big spoon and skim the foam from the blackberry jam.

3. Spoon some jam on a plate and wait until thickened, if not continue boiling and testing. The jam should be thick enough to spoon it into the jars. Few minutes before the jam is ready stir in the orange juice and orange zest and keep stirring until the blackberries mixture has thickened.

4. When the jam is ready, remove the saucepan with the blackberries from the heat and spoon the freshly cooked jam into the sterilized jars up to 1/5 inch from the top.

5. Seal the jars and then process them in a water bath. In a large pot, boil the jars for around 10 minutes and then take them out and leave to cool. Check the lids by pressing them with the finger. In case some of the jars with the blackberry jam are unsealed, place them into the fridge or reprocess the unsealed jars.

## Nutritional Information (1 tbsp):
Calories: 72; Total fat: 0.2 oz; Total carbohydrates: 5 oz; Protein: 4 oz

# Gooseberry & Raspberry Jam

*Prep Time: 40 min. | Makes: 5-6 11 oz jars*

Ingredients:

1.5 lb gooseberries

1.5 lb raspberries

5 cups of sugar

1 tbsp. lemon juice or half tsp. citric acid

How to Prepare:

1. In a big pot, combine berries with the sugar and leave for 2 hours unrefrigerated at room temperature.

2. Boil the berries with the sugar for 40 minutes, stirring until the sugar dissolves and removing the foam and scum from the surface.

3. 5 minutes before the jam is ready mix in the lemon juice or citric acid and keep stirring until the berries jam has thickened.

4. Ladle freshly cooked berries jam into sterilized jars up to 1/4 inch from the top and then seal the jars.

5. Now turn the jars upside down and leave them for at least 5 hours or for overnight to cool completely and only then turn them back. Check the lids by pressing them with the finger. In case some of the jars with the gooseberry jam are unsealed, place them into the fridge or reprocess the unsealed jars.

Nutritional Information (1 tbsp):

Calories: 64; Total fat: 3 oz; Total carbohydrates: 7 oz; Protein: 4 oz

# Orange Blueberry Jam

---

*Prep Time: 25 min.* | *Makes: 5-6 12 oz jars*

---

Ingredients:

4 cups of blueberries, fresh

2 tsp. orange zest, minced

5 cups of sugar

4 tbsp. orange juice

1 tsp. vanilla

How to Prepare:

1. Spoon the blueberries into a food processor or blender and lightly puree them.

2. In a big pot, combine the blueberries, sugar, orange zest, orange juice, and vanilla and boil over medium heat for around 20 minutes, stirring all the time with a spoon until the sugar dissolves. Remove the foam and the scum from the blueberry jam.

3. Spoon some blueberry jam on a plate and wait until thickened, if not continue boiling and testing until thickened.

4. When the jam is ready, remove the pot with the blueberries from the heat and pour freshly cooked jam into sterilized jars up to 1/5 inch from the top.

5. Seal the jars and then place them into the boiling water. In a large pot, boil the jars for around 10 minutes and then take them out and leave to cool. Check the lids by pressing them with the finger. In case some of the jars with the blueberry jam are unsealed, place them into the fridge or reprocess the unsealed jars.

Nutritional Information (1 tbsp):

Calories: 60; Total fat: 2 oz; Total carbohydrates: 4 oz; Protein: 3 oz

# Blueberry Jam with Honey

*Prep Time: 30 min.* | *Makes: 5-6 10 oz jars*

Ingredients:

4 cups of blueberries, fresh or frozen

3 cups of sugar

5 tbsp. honey

5 tbsp. lemon juice

How to Prepare:

1. Defrost the blueberries by leaving them in a bowl at room temperature for at least few hours or place the blueberries in the fridge overnight. Spoon the blueberries into a blender and lightly puree them. In a big saucepan, combine the blueberries, sugar, and honey and boil over medium heat for around 20 minutes, stirring all the time with a spoon until the sugar dissolves. Remove the foam and the scum from the blueberry jam.

2. 5 minutes before the jam is ready mix in the lemon juice and keep stirring until the blueberries jam has thickened. Spoon some blueberry jam on a plate and wait until thickened, if not continue boiling and testing until thickened. When the jam is ready, remove the pot with the blueberries from the heat and pour freshly cooked jam into sterilized jars up to 1/5 inch from the top.

3. Seal the jars and then place them into the boiling water. In a large pot, boil the jars for around 10 minutes and then take them out and leave to cool. Check the lids by pressing them with the finger. In case some of the jars with the blueberry jam are unsealed, place them into the fridge or reprocess the unsealed jars.

Nutritional Information (1 tbsp):
Calories: 59; Total fat: 2 oz; Total carbohydrates: 4 oz; Protein: 1 oz

# Raspberry & Strawberry Jam

---

*Prep Time: 40 min.* | *Makes: 5-6 11 oz jars*

---

## Ingredients:

3 cups of small strawberries, fresh

3 cups of raspberries, fresh

5 cups of sugar

1 tsp. citric acid or lemon juice

## How to Prepare:

1. In a large saucepan, combine the berries with the sugar and leave for at least 5 hours or overnight. (unrefrigerated at room temperature)

2. Bring the berries to the boil and continue boiling over medium heat, stirring all the time until thickened and removing the foam from the surface. Few minutes before the jam is ready mix in the citric acid or lemon juice.

3. Ladle the jam into the sterilized jars up to 1/5 inch from the top.

4. Seal the jars and then flip the jars upside down or boil for around 7-10 minutes and then leave to cool.

## Nutritional Information (1 tbsp):

Calories: 54; Total fat: 3 oz; Total carbohydrates: 7 oz; Protein: 2 oz

# Plum Jelly

*Prep Time: 1 hour | Makes: 6-7 11 oz jars*

Ingredients:

4 lbs plums, pitted

5 cups of sugar

2 tsp. citric acid

How to Prepare:

1. Spoon 1 cup of sugar over the plums and set aside for overnight.

2. Pour some water and boil the plums over the low heat for around 30 minutes, stirring all the time. Then mash the plums with the potato masher and strain the mixture to get 4-5 cups of the juice.

3. In a saucepan, combine the juice with the remaining sugar and boil the juice for 30 minutes until thickened. The jelly should be thick enough to pour it into the jars. Skim the foam from the surface. 10 minutes before the jelly is ready mix in the citric acid.

4. Remove the saucepan from the heat and pour the freshly cooked jelly into the sterilized jars.

5. Turn the jars upside down or boil for around 10 minutes and then leave to cool. Check the lids by pressing them with the finger. In case some of the jars with the plum jelly are unsealed, place them into the fridge or reprocess the unsealed jars.

Nutritional Information (1 tbsp):

Calories: 65; Total fat: 5 oz; Total carbohydrates: 7 oz; Protein: 3 oz

# Lemon Taste Raspberry Jelly

---

*Prep Time: 50 min.* | *Makes: 7-8 10 oz jars*

---

## Ingredients:

25 oz raspberries, fresh

5 cups of sugar

2 medium lemons, halved and squeezed

3 tbsp. pure vanilla extract

## How to Prepare:

1. Spoon 4 tbsp. sugar over the raspberries. Set aside for few hours. Then mash the raspberries using the potato masher.

2. Pour some water and boil the raspberries on a low heat for around 15-20 minutes, stirring all the time. Then strain the raspberries to get 4 cups of the juice.

3. In a saucepan, combine the juice with the sugar and pure vanilla extract. Pour the lemon juice. Boil the raspberry juice for 30 minutes. The jelly should be thick enough to pour it into the jars.

4. Remove the saucepan from the heat and ladle the freshly cooked jelly into the sterilized jars and seal the jars.

5. Flip the jars upside down or boil for around 10 minutes and then leave to cool. Check the lids by pressing them with the finger. In case some of the jars with the raspberry jelly are unsealed, place them into the fridge or reprocess the unsealed jars.

## Nutritional Information (1 tbsp):

Calories: 52; Total fat: 4 oz; Total carbohydrates: 9 oz; Protein: 3 oz

# Alpine Strawberry Orange Jam

---

*Prep Time: 40 min.* | *Makes: 3-4 10 oz jars*

---

## Ingredients:

2-2.5 lb Alpine strawberries

1 tbsp. orange zest, minced

4 cups of sugar

1 tbsp. orange juice

## How to Prepare:

1. Spoon the sugar over the Alpine strawberries and set aside for at least few hours.

2. Boil the Alpine strawberries with the sugar over medium heat for 40 minutes, stirring all the time until thickened. Remove the scum from the surface. Few minutes before the jam is ready mix in the orange zest and orange juice.

3. Pour the Alpine strawberry jam into sterilized jars up to 1/4 inch from the top and seal the jars. Then flip the jars upside down or boil for around 10 minutes and then leave to cool. Check the lids by pressing them with the finger. In case some of the jars with the Alpine strawberry orange jam are unsealed, place them into the fridge or reprocess the unsealed jars.

## Nutritional Information (1 tbsp):

Calories: 53; Total fat: 2 oz; Total carbohydrates: 7 oz; Protein: 3 oz

# Tangerine & Raspberry Jelly

***Prep Time: 50 min. | Makes: 8 10 oz jars***

## Ingredients:

1 lbs tangerines

1 lbs raspberries

1 tbsp. gelatin

5 cups of sugar

2 tsp. citric acid

## How to Prepare:

1. Spoon 1 cup of the sugar over the fruits. Set aside for overnight.

2. Boil the fruits over the low heat for around 20 minutes, stirring all the time. Pour in some water. Then mash the fruits using the potato masher and strain the mixture to get 4-5 cups of the juice.

3. In a saucepan, combine the juice with the remaining sugar and gelatin and boil the juice for 30 minutes until thickened. The jelly should be thick enough to pour it into the jars. Skim the foam from the surface. 10 minutes before the jelly is ready mix in the citric acid.

4. Remove the saucepan from the heat and pour the freshly cooked jelly into the sterilized jars.

5. Turn the jars upside down or boil for around 10 minutes and then leave to cool. Check the lids by pressing them with the finger. In case some of the jars with the jelly are unsealed, place them into the fridge or reprocess the unsealed jars.

## Nutritional Information (1 tbsp):

Calories: 52; Total fat: 6 oz; Total carbohydrates: 9 oz; Protein: 4 oz

# Cherry Jam with Mango and Kiwi

*Prep Time: 40 min. | Makes: 5-6 11 oz jars*

Ingredients:

3 lb cherries, pitted

1 lb mango, peeled and diced

25 oz kiwi's, peeled and diced

5 cups of sugar

1 tbsp. citric acid

How to Prepare:

1. Spoon the sugar over the cherries, mango and kiwi and set aside for few hours. Boil the fruits over medium heat for around 40 minutes, stirring all the time. Remove the foam from the surface and stir in the citric acid.

2. Pour 1 tbs. of fruit jam on a plate and wait until thickened, if not continue boiling and testing. The jam should be thick enough to ladle it into the jars.

4. Remove the saucepan from the heat and ladle the freshly cooked jam into the sterilized jars up to 1/5 inch from the top and seal the jars.

5. Then flip the jars upside down or boil for around 10 minutes and then leave to cool. Check the lids by pressing them with the finger. In case some of the jars with the cherry jam are unsealed, place them into the fridge or reprocess the unsealed jars.

Nutritional Information (1 tbsp):

Calories: 50; Total fat: 7 oz; Total carbohydrates: 6 oz; Protein: 4 oz

# Redcurrant Jelly

*Prep Time: 50 min. | Makes: 6-7 11 oz jars*

Ingredients:

2 lbs redcurrants, fresh

1 tbsp gelatin

5 cups of sugar

How to Prepare:

1. Spoon 4 tbsp. sugar over the redcurrants and set aside for few hours and then crush the berries.

2. Pour some water and boil the redcurrants over the low heat for 15-20 minutes, stirring all the time. Then strain the redcurrants to get 4 cups of the juice.

3. In a saucepan, combine the juice with the sugar and boil the juice for 30 minutes. 10 minutes before the jelly is ready mix in the gelatin. The jelly should be thick enough to ladle it into the jars.

4. Remove the saucepan from the heat and ladle the freshly cooked jelly into the sterilized jars and seal the jars.

5. Flip the jars upside down or boil for around 10 minutes and then leave to cool. Check the lids by pressing them with the finger. In case some of the jars with the redcurrant jelly are unsealed, place them into the fridge or reprocess the unsealed jars.

Nutritional Information (1 tbsp):

Calories: 55; Total fat: 4 oz; Total carbohydrates: 5 oz; Protein: 3 oz

# Blackcurrant Jam

---

*Prep Time: 40 min.* | *Makes: 5-6 11 oz jars*

---

## Ingredients:

4 cups of blackcurrants, fresh

6 cups of sugar

1 tsp. vanilla

## How to Prepare:

1.  Wash the blackcurrants and boil the berries with the sugar over the medium heat for 40 minutes, stirring all the time until thickened. Remove the foam from the surface.

2.  Spoon some jam on a plate and wait until thickened, if not continue boiling and testing. The jam should be thick enough to spoon it into jars. Few minutes before the jam is ready stir in the vanilla.

3.  When the jam is ready, remove the saucepan from the heat and ladle freshly cooked blackcurrant jam into sterilized jars up to 1/5 inch from the top and seal the jars.

4.  Flip the jars with the blackcurrant jam upside down or boil for around 10 minutes and then leave to cool. Check the lids by pressing them with the finger. In case some of the jars with the blackcurrant jam are unsealed, place them into the fridge or reprocess the unsealed jars.

## Nutritional Information (1 tbsp):

Calories: 54; Total fat: 5 oz; Total carbohydrates: 8 oz; Protein: 2 oz

# Plum and Blackcurrant Jelly

*Prep Time: 55 min. | Makes: 7-8 12 oz jars*

## Ingredients:

7 cups of blackcurrants, fresh

1 lbs plums, pitted

4 cups of sugar

1 tsp. citric acid

1 tsp. vanilla

## How to Prepare:

1. Spoon 4 tbsp. sugar over the blackcurrants and plums. Set aside for few hours and then mash the berries using the potatoes masher.

2. Pour some water and boil the blackcurrants and plums over low heat for 20-25 minutes, stirring all the time. Then strain the blackcurrants and plums to get 4-5 cups of the juice.

3. In a saucepan, combine the juice with the sugar and vanilla and boil the juice for 30 minutes. The jelly should be thick enough to ladle it into the jars. Remove the foam from the surface.

4. Remove the saucepan from the heat and ladle the freshly cooked jelly into the sterilized jars and seal the jars.

5. Flip the jars upside down or boil for around 10 minutes and then leave to cool. In case some of the jars with the blackcurrant jelly are unsealed, place them into the fridge or reprocess the unsealed jars.

Nutritional Information (1 tbsp):

Calories: 54; Total fat: 5 oz; Total carbohydrates: 8 oz; Protein: 4 oz

# Baked Vanilla Plum Jam

*Prep Time: 2 hours | Makes around 7 11 oz jars*

Ingredients:

6 lb plums, stoned and halved

1 cup of water

5 cups of sugar

3 tsp. vanilla

baking spray or unsalted butter

How to Prepare:

1. Combine the stoned and halved plums with the sugar and preheat the oven to 300°-360° Fahrenheit and then coat the baking pan with the baking spray or unsalted butter.

2. Pour one cup of water and mix in three teaspoons vanilla and bake the plums for around 1.5-2 hours until thickened and gelled enough to spoon the plum jam into the jars. If the vanilla plum jam is not gelled enough continue baking and testing every five or ten minutes. The plum jam should be gelled enough to spoon it into the jars.

3. Spoon the freshly baked vanilla plum jam into the sterilized and hot jars up to 1/5 inch from the top and seal the jars.

4. Flip the jars upside down or boil for around 10 minutes and then leave to cool. Check the lids by pressing them with the finger. In case some of the jars with the vanilla and plum jam are unsealed, place them into the fridge or reprocess the unsealed jars.

Nutritional Information (1 tbsp):

Calories: 58; Total fat: 7 oz; Total carbohydrates: 8 oz; Protein: 3 oz

# Baked Pear Jam

---

*Prep Time: 50 min.│Makes around 7 11 oz jars*

---

Ingredients:

5 lb sweet pears, peeled and cubed

4 cups of sugar

5 tbsp. lemon juice

1 tbsp. cinnamon

baking spray or butter

## How to Prepare:

1. Wash and peel the pears and then cube them. Spoon the sugar and pour the lemon juice over the pears and set aside for around 2 to 3 hours unrefrigerated at room temperature.

2. Preheat the oven to 300°-350° Fahrenheit and then coat the baking pan with the baking spray or butter.

3. Spoon the cinnamon over the pears. Then bake the pears with the sugar, lemon juice, and cinnamon for around 40 minutes until thickened and gelled enough, if not continue baking and testing every five to ten minutes. The pear jam should be gelled enough to ladle it into the jars.

4. When the pear jam is ready ladle the freshly baked jam into the sterilized and hot jars up to 1/4 inch from the top and then seal the jars.

5. Flip the jars upside down or boil for around 10 minutes and then leave to cool. Check the lids by pressing them with the finger. In case some of the jars with the pear jam are unsealed, place them into the fridge or reprocess the unsealed jars.

Nutritional Information (1 tbsp):

Calories: 45; Total fat: 2 oz; Total carbohydrates: 4 oz; Protein: 2oz

# Baked Pears & Orange Jam

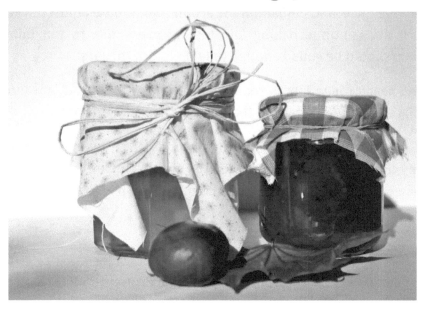

*Prep Time: 50 min. | Makes around 7 11 oz jars*

Ingredients:

6 lb sweet pears, peeled and cubed

3 cups of sugar

4 tbsp. orange zest, minced

1 glass of orange juice

1 tbsp. cinnamon

baking spray or butter

How to Prepare:

1.  Wash and peel the pears and then cube them. Spoon the sugar and pour one cup of the orange juice over the pears and set aside for around 2 to 3 hours unrefrigerated at room temperature.

2.  Preheat the oven to 300°-350° Fahrenheit and then coat the baking pan with the baking spray or butter.

3. Spoon the cinnamon and orange zest over the pears. Then bake the pears with the sugar, orange juice, and cinnamon for around 50 minutes until thickened and gelled enough, if not continue baking and testing every five to ten minutes. The pear orange jam should be gelled enough to ladle it into the jars.

4. When the pear orange jam is ready ladle the freshly baked jam into the sterilized and hot jars up to 1/5 inch from the top and then seal the jars.

5. Flip the jars upside down or boil for around 10 minutes and then leave to cool. Check the lids by pressing them with the finger. In case some of the jars with the pear orange jam are unsealed, place them into the fridge or reprocess the unsealed jars.

**Nutritional Information (1 tbsp):**

Calories: 48; Total fat: 3 oz; Total carbohydrates: 5 oz; Protein: 2 oz

# Vanilla Apple Jam

---

*Prep Time: 40 min.│Makes around 5-6 10 oz jars*

---

Ingredients:

10 big and sweet Fuji apples, peeled and cubed

5 cups of sugar

3 tsp. vanilla

2 tsp. citric acid

How to Prepare:

1. Wash and peel the Fuji apples and then cube them. Spoon the sugar and citric acid over the apples and set aside for around 1 to 2 hours unrefrigerated at room temperature or place in the fridge for overnight.

2. Boil the apples with the sugar over medium heat for around 40 minutes, stirring all the time.

3. Few minutes before the apple jam is ready mix in the vanilla. Remove the saucepan from the heat and ladle freshly cooked jam into sterilized jars up to 1/5 inch from the top.

4. Flip the jars with the vanilla apple jam upside down or boil for around 10 minutes and then leave to cool. Check the lids by pressing them with the finger. In case some of the jars with the vanilla apple jam are unsealed, place them into the fridge or reprocess the unsealed jars.

Nutritional Information (1 tbsp):

Calories: 46; Total fat: 5 oz; Total carbohydrates: 8 oz; Protein: 3 oz

# Baked Apple Orange Jam

---

*Prep Time: 50 min.│Makes around 7 11 oz jars*

---

Ingredients:

7-8 lb sweet Fuji or Gala apples, peeled and cubed

5 cups of sugar

2 tbsp. orange zest, minced

one cup of orange juice

1 tbsp. cinnamon

baking spray or butter

How to Prepare:

1. Wash and peel Fuji or Gala apples and then cube them. Spoon the sugar and pour one cup of the orange juice over the apples and then set aside for around 1 to 3 hours unrefrigerated at room temperature.

2. Preheat the oven to 300°-350° Fahrenheit and then coat the baking pan with the baking spray or butter.

3. Spoon the cinnamon and orange zest over the cubed apples. Then bake the apples with the sugar, orange juice, and cinnamon for around 50 minutes until thickened and gelled enough, if not gelled enough continue baking and testing every five to ten minutes. The apple orange jam should be gelled enough to spoon it into the jars.

4. When the apple orange jam is ready spoon the freshly baked jam into the sterilized and hot jars up to 1/5 inch from the top and then seal the jars.

5. Flip the jars upside down or boil for around 10 minutes and then leave to cool. Check the lids by pressing them with the finger. In case some of the jars with the apple orange jam are unsealed, place them into the fridge or reprocess the unsealed jars.

Nutritional Information (1 tbsp):

Calories: 51; Total fat: 2 oz; Total carbohydrates: 6 oz; Protein: 2 oz

# Cinnamon Apple Jam

*Prep Time: 40 min. | Makes around 4 10 oz jars*

Ingredients:

8 big and sweet Gala apples, peeled and cubed

5 cups of sugar

2 tsp. Cinnamon

2 tsp. citric acid

How to Prepare:

1. Wash and peel the apples and then cube them. Spoon the sugar and citric acid over the apples and set aside for around 3 to 4 hours unrefrigerated at room temperature or place in the fridge for overnight.

2. Boil the apples with the sugar over medium heat for around 40 minutes, stirring all the time.

3. Few minutes before the apple jam is ready stir in the cinnamon. Remove the saucepan from the heat and ladle freshly cooked jam into sterilized jars up to 1/5 inch from the top.

4. Flip the jars with the cinnamon apple jam upside down or boil for around 10 minutes and then leave to cool. Check the lids by pressing them with the finger. In case some of the jars with the cinnamon apple jam are unsealed, place them into the fridge or reprocess the unsealed jars.

Nutritional Information (1 tbsp):
Calories: 46; Total fat: 4 oz; Total carbohydrates: 8 oz; Protein: 2 oz

# Orange Peach Jam

---

## *Prep Time: 40 min. | Makes around 6 10 oz jars*

---

Ingredients:

4 lb peaches, peeled and sliced

5 cups of sugar

2 tsp. orange zest, minced

4 tbsp. orange juice

How to Prepare:

1. Boil the peaches with the sugar over medium heat for around 40 minutes, stirring all the time until the sugar dissolves. Remove the foam from the surface.

2. Pour some orange peach jam on a plate and check if it has gelled enough, by pressing with the finger, if not continue boiling and testing every five or ten minutes. The jam should be thick enough to spoon it into the jars. Few minutes before the jam is ready mix in the orange zest and orange juice and keep stirring. When the jam is ready, remove the saucepan from the heat and ladle freshly cooked orange peach jam into the sterilized jars up to 1/5 inch from the top and seal the jars.

3. Flip the jars with the orange peach jam upside down or process them in a water bath. In a large pot, boil the jars for around 10 minutes and then take them out and leave to cool. Check the lids by pressing them with the finger. In case some of the jars with the orange peach jam are unsealed, place them into the fridge or reprocess the unsealed jars.

Nutritional Information (1 tbsp):
Calories: 54; Total fat: 4 oz; Total carbohydrates: 7 oz; Protein: 3 oz

# Grandma's Raspberry Jam

*Prep Time: 40 min.* | *Makes: 5-6 10 oz jars*

Ingredients:

3.5 lb fresh raspberries

2 cups of brown sugar

2 cups of white, table sugar

3 tbsp. lemon juice, squeezed

1 tsp. vanilla

How to Prepare:

1. In a bowl, combine the brown sugar and white sugar with vanilla and mix well.

2. Then place the raspberries into a big saucepan and spoon the sugar-vanilla mixture on top and leave for at least 5 hours unrefrigerated at room temperature or place in the fridge overnight.

3. In the same saucepan boil the raspberries and sugar-vanilla mixture over high heat for around 10 minutes, stirring all the time with a spoon until sugar dissolves.

4. Then reduce the heat and continue to boil for around 30 minutes but don't forget to skim the foam from the raspberries.

5. Pour the lemon juice and keep stirring until the raspberries mixture has thickened.

6.  Remove the saucepan with the raspberries from the heat and pour freshly cooked jam into sterilized jars up to 1/5 inch from the top.

7.  Seal the jars and then turn the jars upside down. Leave them for overnight to cool completely and only then turn them back.

8.  Or you can do it more traditionally by placing the jars into the water bath and boiling for around 7-10 minutes and then leaving to cool. Check the lids by pressing them with the finger. In case some of the jars with the raspberry jam are unsealed, place them into the fridge or reprocess the unsealed jars.

**Nutritional Information (1 tbsp):**

Calories: 60; Total fat: 5 oz; Total carbohydrates: 8 oz; Protein: 3 oz

# Coconut Raspberry Jam

*Prep Time: 40 min. | Makes: 5-6 10 oz jars*

**Ingredients:**

8 cups of fresh raspberries

3 tbsp. shredded coconut

5 cups of sugar

2 tbsp. coconut butter

1.5 tbsp. citric acid

**How to Prepare:**

1. In a large pot, combine the raspberries with the sugar and leave for at least 5 hours unrefrigerated at room temperature or place in the fridge overnight.

2. In the same pot boil the raspberries, sugar and coconut butter over medium heat for around 40 minutes, stirring all the time with a spoon until sugar dissolves and don't forget to skim the foam from the raspberries.

3. 5 min. before the jam is ready mix in the shredded coconut and citric acid and keep stirring until the raspberries mixture has gelled.

4. Remove the saucepan with the raspberries from the heat and pour freshly cooked jam into sterilized jars up to 1/5 inch from the top.

5. Water bath: seal the jars and boil them for around 10 minutes and then leave to cool. Check the lids by pressing them with the finger. In case some of the jars with the coconut and raspberry jam are unsealed, place them into the fridge or reprocess the unsealed jars.

**Nutritional Information (1 tbsp):**

Calories: 95; Total fat: 0.2 oz; Total carbohydrates: 5.2 oz; Protein: 0.7 oz

# Strawberry Jam

---

*Prep Time: 35 min.* | *Makes: 7-8 12 oz jars*

---

Ingredients:

5 lb fresh strawberries, halved

6.5 cups of sugar

3 tbsp. lemon juice, freshly squeezed

1 tsp. cinnamon

How to Prepare:

1. In a saucepan, combine the sugar and 1.5 cup of water and bring the mixture to the boil.

2. Add the strawberries and boil over medium heat for around 30 minutes, stirring all the time with a spoon until the sugar dissolves and don't forget to skim the foam from the strawberry jam.

3. 5 min. before the jam is ready mix in the lemon juice and cinnamon and keep stirring until the strawberries mixture has thickened and gelled. Spoon some jam on a plate and wait until thickened, if not continue boiling and testing every 5 minutes.

4. Remove the saucepan with the strawberries from the heat and spoon freshly cooked jam into sterilized jars up to 1/5 inch from the top.

5. Seal the jars and then turn the jars upside down. Leave them for overnight to cool completely and only then turn them back. Check the lids by pressing them with the finger. In case some of the jars with the strawberry jam are unsealed, place them into the fridge or reprocess the unsealed jars.

Nutritional Information (1 tbsp):

Calories: 90; Total fat: 2 oz; Total carbohydrates: 4 oz; Protein: 0.9 oz

# Sugar-Free Strawberry Jam

---

*Prep Time: 50 min.* | *Makes: 7-8 10 oz jars*

---

## Ingredients:

5 lb fresh and sweet strawberries

4 tbsp. granulated erythritol

1 tbsp. citric acid

1 tsp. vanilla


## How to Prepare:

1. Place the strawberries into a big saucepan and spoon the erythritol citric acid and vanilla on top.

2. Boil the strawberries mixture over medium heat for around 30 minutes, stirring all the time until erythritol dissolves. Remove the foam from the strawberries jam while boiling. Keep stirring until the strawberries jam has gelled.

3. Remove the saucepan with the strawberries from the heat and pour freshly cooked jam into sterilized jars up to 1/5 inch from the top.

4. Seal the jars and then turn the jars upside down. Leave them for overnight to cool completely and only then turn them back. Check the lids by pressing them with the finger. In case some of the jars with the strawberry jam are unsealed, place them into the fridge or reprocess the unsealed jars.

## Nutritional Information (1 tbsp):

Calories: 50; Total fat: 4 oz; Total carbohydrates: 7 oz; Protein: 3 oz

# Orange Strawberry Jam

*Prep Time: 40 min. | Makes: 6-7 11 oz jars*

Ingredients:

4 lb fresh and small strawberries

2 tbsp. orange zest, minced

5.5 cups of sugar

2 tbsp. orange juice, freshly squeezed

How to Prepare:

1. In a saucepan, combine the sugar and 1 cup of water and bring the mixture to the boil.

2. Add the strawberries and boil over medium heat for around 40 minutes, stirring all the time with a spoon until the sugar dissolves and don't forget to skim the foam from the strawberry jam.

3. 5-7 min. before the jam is ready mix in the orange juice and orange zest and keep stirring until the strawberries mixture has thickened. Spoon some jam on a plate and wait until thickened, if not continue boiling and testing.

4. When the jam is ready, remove the saucepan with the strawberries from the heat and spoon freshly cooked jam into sterilized jars up to 1/5 inch from the top.

5.  Seal the jars and then turn the jars upside down. Leave them for overnight to cool completely and only then turn them back. Check the lids by pressing them with the finger. In case some of the jars are unsealed, place them into the fridge or reprocess the unsealed jars.

**Nutritional Information (1 tbsp):**

Calories: 69; Total fat: 2 oz; Total carbohydrates: 5 oz; Protein: 2 oz

# Grandma's Gooseberry Jam

*Prep Time: 40 min.* | *Makes: 5-6 11 oz jars*

Ingredients:

1.5 lb gooseberries

1.5 lb raspberries

5 cups of sugar

1 tbsp. lemon juice or half tsp. citric acid

How to Prepare:

1. In a big pot, combine berries with the sugar and leave for 2 hours unrefrigerated at room temperature.

2. Boil the berries with the sugar for 40 minutes, stirring until the sugar dissolves and removing the foam and scum from the surface.

3. 5 minutes before the jam is ready mix in the lemon juice or citric acid and keep stirring until the berries jam has thickened.

4. Ladle freshly cooked berries jam into sterilized jars up to 1/4 inch from the top and then seal the jars.

5. Now turn the jars upside down and leave them for at least 5 hours or for overnight to cool completely and only then turn them back. Check the lids by pressing them

with the finger. In case some of the jars with the gooseberry jam are unsealed, place them into the fridge or reprocess the unsealed jars.

**Nutritional Information (1 tbsp):**

Calories: 62; Total fat: 2 oz; Total carbohydrates: 2.3 oz; Protein: 1 oz

# Lemon-Peach Jam

---

*Prep Time: 40 min.* | *Makes: 4-5 12 oz jars*

---

Ingredients:

4 lb peaches, washed and sliced

3 tbsp. lemon zest, minced

5 cups of sugar

4 tbsp. lemon juice

How to Prepare:

1. In a large saucepan, combine the peaches and sugar and boil over medium heat for around 40 minutes, stirring all the time with a spoon until the sugar dissolves. Take a big spoon and remove the scum from the surface.

2. Spoon some jam on a plate and wait until thickened, if not continue boiling and testing. The jam should be thick enough to spoon it into jars. Few minutes before the jam is ready, stir in the lemon juice and lemon zest and keep stirring until the peach mixture has thickened.

3. When the jam is ready, remove the saucepan from the heat and spoon freshly cooked jam into sterilized jars up to 1/5 inch from the top.

4. Seal the jars and then place them into the boiling water. In a large pot, boil the jars for around 10 minutes and then take them out and leave to cool. Check the lids by pressing them with the finger. In case some of the jars with the lemon peach jam are unsealed, place them into the fridge or reprocess the unsealed jars.

Nutritional Information (1 tbsp):

Calories: 69; Total fat: 2 oz; Total carbohydrates: 4.6 oz; Protein: 2 oz

# Mom's Blueberry Jam

---

*Prep Time: 30 min.* | *Makes: 8 12 oz jars*

---

## Ingredients:

6 cups of blueberries, fresh or frozen

6 cups of sugar

2 tsp. pure vanilla extract

2 tsp. citric acid

## How to Prepare:

1. Defrost the blueberries by leaving them in a bowl at room temperature for at least few hours or place the blueberries in the fridge overnight.

2. Spoon the blueberries into a blender and lightly puree them.

3. In a big saucepan, combine the blueberries, sugar, and vanilla and boil over medium heat for around 20 minutes, stirring all the time with a spoon until the sugar dissolves. Remove the foam and the scum from the blueberry jam.

4. 5 minutes before the jam is ready mix in the citric acid and keep stirring until the blueberries jam has thickened. Spoon some blueberry jam on a plate and wait until thickened, if not continue boiling and testing until thickened.

5. When the jam is ready, remove the pot with the blueberries from the heat and pour freshly cooked jam into sterilized jars up to 1/5 inch from the top.

6. Seal the jars and then place them into the boiling water. In a large pot, boil the jars for around 10 minutes and then take them out and leave to cool. Check the lids by pressing them with the finger. In case some of the jars with the blueberry jam are unsealed, place them into the fridge or reprocess the unsealed jars.

## Nutritional Information (1 tbsp):

Calories: 62; Total fat: 2 oz; Total carbohydrates: 4 oz; Protein: 3 oz

# Semi-Sweet Blueberry Jam

---

***Prep Time: 40 min.*** | ***Makes: 5-6 10 oz jars***

---

Ingredients:

5 cups of blueberries, fresh

1 cup of white sugar

2 tbsp. gelatin

2 tsp. citric acid

1 tsp. vanilla

How to Prepare:

1. Combine the gelatin with the warm water. Pour into the large saucepan, combine the blueberries and sugar and boil over medium heat for around 40 minutes, stirring all the time until the sugar dissolves. Take a big spoon and remove the foam and the scum from the surface.

2. Spoon some jam on a plate and wait until thickened, if not continue boiling and testing. The jam should be thick enough to spoon it into jars. Few minutes before the jam is ready stir in the citric acid and vanilla.

3. When the blueberry jam is ready, remove the saucepan from the heat and spoon freshly cooked jam into sterilized jars up to 1/5 inch from the top and seal the jars.

4. Turn the jars upside down and leave them for at least 5 hours or for overnight to cool completely and only then turn them back. Check the lids by pressing them with the finger. In case some of the jars with the blueberry jam are unsealed, place them into the fridge or reprocess the unsealed jars.

Nutritional Information (1 tbsp):

Calories: 50; Total fat: 2 oz; Total carbohydrates: 5 oz; Protein: 3 oz

# Lemon-Blueberry Jam

---

*Prep Time: 25 min.│ Makes: 5-6 12 oz jars*

---

Ingredients:

4 cups of blueberries, fresh

2 tsp. lemon zest, minced

5 cups of sugar

4 tbsp. lemon juice

1 tsp. vanilla

How to Prepare:

1. Spoon the blueberries into a food processor or blender and lightly puree them.

2. In a big pot, combine the blueberries, sugar, lemon zest, lemon juice, and vanilla and boil over medium heat for around 20 minutes, stirring all the time with a spoon until the sugar dissolves. Remove the foam and the scum from the blueberry jam.

3. Spoon some blueberry jam on a plate and wait until thickened, if not continue boiling and testing until thickened.

4. When the jam is ready, remove the pot with the blueberries from the heat and pour freshly cooked jam into sterilized jars up to 1/5 inch from the top.

5. Seal the jars and then place them into the boiling water. In a large pot, boil the jars for around 10 minutes and then take them out and leave to cool. Check the lids by pressing them with the finger. In case some of the jars with the blueberry jam are unsealed, place them into the fridge or reprocess the unsealed jars.

Nutritional Information (1 tbsp):

Calories: 60; Total fat: 2 oz; Total carbohydrates: 3 oz; Protein: 1 oz

# Forest Berry Jam

---

*Prep Time: 40 min.* | *Makes: 5-6 11 oz jars*

---

Ingredients:

2 cups of blueberries, fresh

2 cups of Alpine strawberries, fresh

1 cup of raspberries, fresh

5 cups of sugar

2 tsp. citric acid

1 tsp. vanilla

How to Prepare:

1. In a large saucepan, combine the berries with the sugar and leave for at least 5 hours or overnight. (unrefrigerated at room temperature)

2. Boil the berries over medium heat for around 40 minutes, stirring all the time until the sugar dissolves. Remove the foam and the scum from the surface.

3. Spoon some jam on a plate and wait until thickened, if not continue boiling and testing. The jam should be thick enough to spoon it into jars. Few minutes before the jam is ready stir in the citric acid and vanilla.

4. When the forest berries jam is ready, remove the saucepan from the heat and spoon freshly cooked jam into sterilized jars up to 1/5 inch from the top and seal the jars.

5. Turn the jars upside down and leave them for at least 5 hours or overnight to cool completely and only then turn them back. Check the lids by pressing them with the finger. In case some of jars with the forest berries are unsealed, place them into the fridge or reprocess the unsealed jars.

Nutritional Information (1 tbsp):

Calories: 60; Total fat: 3 oz; Total carbohydrates: 1.2 oz; Protein: 2 oz

# Alpine Strawberry Jam

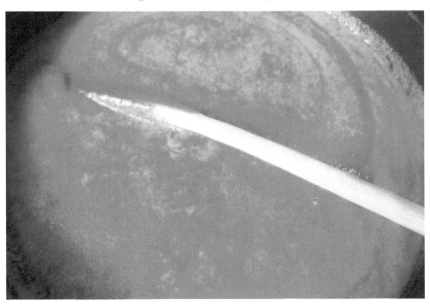

*Prep Time: 40 min.* | *Makes: 3-4 10 oz jars*

Ingredients:

2-2.5 lb Alpine strawberries

4 cups of sugar

1 tsp. citric acid

How to Prepare:

1. Spoon the sugar over the Alpine strawberries and set aside for at least few hours.

2. Boil the Alpine strawberries with the sugar over medium heat for 40 minutes, stirring all the time until thickened. Remove the scum from the surface. Few minutes before the jam is ready mix in the citric acid.

3. Pour the Alpine strawberries jam into sterilized jars up to 1/5 inch from the top.

4. Seal the jars and then flip the jars upside down or boil for around 7-10 minutes and then leave to cool. Check the lids by pressing them with the finger. In case some of the jars with the Alpine strawberry jam are unsealed, place them into the fridge or reprocess the unsealed jars.

Nutritional Information (1 tbsp):

Calories: 52; Total fat: 2 oz; Total carbohydrates: 4 oz; Protein: 2 oz

# Orange Cherry Jam

---

*Prep Time: 20 min.* | *Makes: 4-5 11 oz jars*

---

## Ingredients:

4 cups of cherries, washed and pitted

3 tbsp. orange zest, minced

4 cups of sugar

3 tbsp. orange juice

## How to Prepare:

1. Spoon the sugar over the cherries and pour few glasses of water, and then boil the cherries over low heat for 15-20 minutes, stirring all the time.

2. Remove the foam from the surface and stir in the orange zest and orange juice.

3. Remove the saucepan from the heat and ladle the freshly cooked jam into the sterilized jars and seal them.

4. Flip the jars upside down or boil for around 10 minutes and then leave to cool. Check the lids by pressing them with the finger. In case some of the jars are unsealed, place them into the fridge or reprocess the unsealed jars.

## Nutritional Information (1 tbsp):

Calories: 57; Total fat: 3 oz; Total carbohydrates: 6 oz; Protein: 2 oz

# Grandma's Cherry Jam

*Prep Time: 40 min.* | *Makes: 5-6 11 oz jars*

Ingredients:

3 lb cherries, pitted

5 cups of sugar

1 tbsp. citric acid

How to Prepare:

1. Spoon the sugar over the cherries and set aside for few hours. Boil the cherries over medium heat for around 40 minutes, stirring all the time. Remove the foam from the surface and stir in the citric acid.

2. Pour one tablespoon cherry jam on a plate and wait until thickened, if not continue boiling and testing. The jam should be thick enough to ladle it into the jars.

3. Remove the saucepan from the heat and ladle the freshly cooked jam into the sterilized jars up to 1/5 inch from the top and seal the jars.

4. Then flip the jars upside down or boil for around 10 minutes and then leave to cool. Check the lids by pressing them with the finger. In case some of the jars with the cherry jam are unsealed, place them into the fridge or reprocess the unsealed jars.

Nutritional Information (1 tbsp):

Calories: 49; Total fat: 4 oz; Total carbohydrates: 8 oz; Protein: 2 oz

# Baked Cherry Jam

*Prep Time: 1 hour* | *Makes: 6-7 11 oz jars*

## Ingredients:

8 cups of cherries, pitted

4 cups of sugar

1 tbsp. Cinnamon

## How to Prepare:

1. Preheat the oven to 300°-350° Fahrenheit, combine the cherries with the sugar and mix in some water and cinnamon and bake the cherries for around 1-1.5 hours until gelled, if not continue baking. The cherry jam should be gelled enough to spoon it into the jars.

2. Spoon the freshly baked jam into the sterilized jars up to 1/5 inch from the top and seal the jars.

3. Flip the jars upside down or boil for around 10 minutes and then leave to cool. Check the lids by pressing them with the finger. In case some of the jars with the cherry jam are unsealed, place them into the fridge or reprocess the unsealed jars.

## Nutritional Information (1 tbsp):

Calories: 57; Total fat: 2 oz; Total carbohydrates: 7 oz; Protein: 1 oz

# Grandma's Blackcurrant Jelly

*Prep Time: 50 min.* | *Makes: 6-7 11 oz jars*

Ingredients:

6 cups of blackcurrants, fresh

4 cups of sugar

1 tsp. citric acid

1 tsp. vanilla

How to Prepare:

1. Spoon 4 tbsp. sugar over the blackcurrants and set aside for few hours and then crush the berries.

2. Pour some water and boil the blackcurrants over low heat for 15-20 minutes, stirring all the time. Then strain the blackcurrants to get 4-5 cups of the juice.

3. In a saucepan, combine the juice with the sugar and vanilla and boil the juice for 30 minutes. The jelly should be thick enough to ladle it into the jars. Remove the foam from the surface.

4. Remove the saucepan from the heat and ladle the freshly cooked jelly into the sterilized jars and seal the jars.

5. Flip the jars upside down or boil for around 10 minutes and then leave to cool. In case some of the jars with the blackcurrant jelly are unsealed, place them into the fridge or reprocess the unsealed jars.

**Nutritional Information (1 tbsp):**

Calories: 55; Total fat: 1 oz; Total carbohydrates: 5 oz; Protein: 2 oz

# Orange Blackcurrant Jam

*Prep Time: 40 min.* | *Makes: 6-7 11 oz jars*

Ingredients:

2.5 lb blackcurrants, fresh

2 tbsp. orange zest, minced

5 cups of sugar

2 tbsp. orange juice

How to Prepare:

1. Boil the blackcurrants with the sugar over medium heat for 40 minutes, stirring all the time and removing the foam from the surface.

2. Spoon some jam on a plate and wait until thickened, if not continue boiling and testing until gelled. The jam should be thick enough to ladle it into the jars. 10 minutes before the jam is ready mix in the orange zest and orange juice.

3. Remove the saucepan from the heat and ladle freshly cooked jam into sterilized jars up to 1/5 inch from the top and seal the jars.

4. Flip the jars with the jam upside down or boil for around 10 minutes and then leave to cool. In case some of the jars with the blackcurrant jam are unsealed, place them into the fridge or reprocess the unsealed jars.

Nutritional Information (1 tbsp):

Calories: 53; Total fat: 1 oz; Total carbohydrates: 4 oz; Protein: 1 oz

# Orange Redcurrant Jelly

*Prep Time: 50 min.│Makes: 6-7 11 oz jars*

Ingredients:

6 cups of redcurrants, fresh

3 tbsp. orange zest, minced

5 cups of sugar

3 tbsp. orange juice

How to Prepare:

1. Spoon 4 tbsp. sugar over the redcurrants and set aside for few hours and then crush the berries.

2. Pour some water and boil the redcurrants over low heat for 15-20 minutes, stirring all the time. Then strain the redcurrants to get 4 cups of the juice.

3. In a saucepan, combine the juice with the sugar and boil the juice for 30 minutes. The jelly should be thick enough to ladle it into the jars. Remove the foam from the surface. 10 minutes before the jelly is ready mix in the orange zest and orange juice.

4. Remove the saucepan from the heat and ladle the freshly cooked jelly into the sterilized jars and seal the jars.

5. Flip the jars upside down or boil for around 10 minutes and then leave to cool. Check the lids by pressing them with the finger. In case some of the jars with the redcurrant jelly are unsealed, place them into the fridge or reprocess the unsealed jars.

**Nutritional Information (1 tbsp):**

Calories: 56; Total fat: 1 oz; Total carbohydrates: 7 oz; Protein: 2 oz

# Quince Redcurrant Jelly

---

*Prep Time: 1 hour* | *Makes: 6-7 11 oz jars*

---

Ingredients:

4 lb quinces, halved

2 cups of redcurrants, fresh

5 cups of sugar

1 tsp. citric acid

How to Prepare:

1.  Slice the quinces and spoon 1 cup of sugar over them and set aside for overnight.

2.  Pour 5 cups of water and boil the quinces with the redcurrants over low heat for 30 minutes, stirring all the time. Then strain the quince mixture to get 4-5 cups of the juice.

3.  In a saucepan, combine the juice with the remaining sugar and boil the juice for 30 minutes until thickened. The jelly should be thick enough to pour it into the jars. Skim the foam from the surface. 10 minutes before the jelly is ready mix in the citric acid.

4.  Remove the saucepan from the heat and pour the freshly cooked jelly into the sterilized jars.

5.  Turn the jars upside down or boil for around 10 minutes and then leave to cool. Check the lids by pressing them with the finger. In case some of the jars with the redcurrant jelly are unsealed, place them into the fridge or reprocess the unsealed jars.

Nutritional Information (1 tbsp):

Calories: 57; Total fat: 2 oz; Total carbohydrates: 8 oz; Protein: 1.5 oz

# Quince Jelly

*Prep Time: 1 hour* | *Makes: 6-7 11 oz jars*

Ingredients:

8 cups of quinces, halved

6 cups of sugar

1 tsp. citric acid

1 tsp. cinnamon

How to Prepare:

1. Slice the quinces and spoon 1 cup of sugar over them and set aside for overnight.

2. Heat 5 cups of water and boil the quinces over medium heat for 30 minutes, stirring all the time. Then strain the quince mixture to get 4-5 cups of the juice.

3. In a saucepan, combine the juice with the remaining sugar and boil the juice for 30 minutes until thickened. The jelly should be thick enough to pour it into the jars. Skim the foam from the surface. 10 minutes before the jelly is ready mix in the citric acid.

4. Remove the saucepan from the heat and pour the freshly cooked jelly into the sterilized jars.

5. Turn the jars upside down or boil for around 10 minutes and then leave to cool. Check the lids by pressing them with the finger. In case some of the jars with the quince jelly are unsealed, place them into the fridge or reprocess the unsealed jars.

Nutritional Information (1 tbsp):

Calories: 49; Total fat: 2 oz; Total carbohydrates: 8 oz; Protein: 1 oz

# Orange Quince Jam

---

*Prep Time: 50 min.* | *Makes: 6-7 11 oz jars*

---

Ingredients:

8 cups of quinces, halved

6 cups of sugar

1 tbsp. orange zest, minced

4 tbsp. orange juice

1 tsp. vanilla

How to Prepare:

1. Process the quinces in a food processor or blender and boil with the sugar and few cups of water over medium heat for around 50 minutes, stirring all the time until gelled. Remove the foam from the surface.

2. Spoon some jam on a plate and wait until thickened and gelled, if not continue boiling and testing. The jam should be thick enough to spoon it into the jars. 5 minutes before the jam is ready stir in the orange zest and orange juice.

3. When the quince jam is ready, remove the saucepan from the heat and ladle freshly cooked jam into sterilized jars up to 1/5 inch from the top to seal the jars.

4. Then process the jars with the jam in a water bath. In a large pot, boil the jars for around 10 minutes and then take them out and leave to cool. Check the lids by pressing them with the finger. In case some of the jars with the quince jam are unsealed, place them into the fridge or reprocess the unsealed jars.

Nutritional Information (1 tbsp):

Calories: 57; Total fat: 2 oz; Total carbohydrates: 3 oz; Protein: 1 oz

# Lemon Quince Jam

*Prep Time: 50 min.│Makes: 6-7 11 oz jars*

Ingredients:

8 cups of quinces, halved

3 cups of sugar

3 cups of brown sugar

1 tbsp. lemon zest, minced

4 tbsp. lemon or lime juice

1 tsp. vanilla

How to Prepare:

1. Process the quinces in a food processor or blender and boil with the sugar and few cups of water over medium heat for around 50 minutes, stirring all the time until gelled. Remove the foam and scum from the surface.

2. Pour some jam on a plate and check if it has gelled enough, by pressing with the finger, if not continue boiling and testing. The jam should be thick enough to ladle it into the jars. 5 minutes before the jam is ready mix in the lemon zest and lemon or lime juice.

3. When the quince jam is ready, remove the saucepan from the heat and spoon freshly cooked jam into sterilized jars up to 1/5 inch from the top to seal the jars.

4. Then process the jars with the jam in a water bath. In a large pot, boil the jars for around 10 minutes and then take them out and leave to cool. Check the lids by pressing them with the finger. In case some of the jars with the quince jam are unsealed, place them into the fridge or reprocess the unsealed jars.

**Nutritional Information (1 tbsp):**

Calories: 56; Total fat: 2 oz; Total carbohydrates: 7 oz; Protein: 2 oz

# Quince Jam

*Prep Time: 50 min. | Makes: 6-7 11 oz jars*

Ingredients:

5 lb quinces, halved and sliced

4.5 cups of sugar

2 tbsp. liquid honey

1 tsp. citric acid

How to Prepare:

1. Slice the quinces in a food processor and boil with the sugar and few cups of water over medium heat for around 50 minutes, stirring all the time until gelled. Remove the foam and scum from the surface.

2. Pour some jam on a plate and check if it has gelled enough, by pressing with the finger, if not continue boiling and testing. The jam should be thick enough to ladle it into the jars. 5 minutes before the jam is ready mix in the citric acid and liquid honey.

3. When the quince jam is ready, remove the saucepan from the heat and spoon freshly cooked jam into sterilized jars up to 1/5 inch from the top to seal the jars.

4. Then process the jars with the jam in a water bath. In a large pot, boil the jars for around 10 minutes and then take them out and leave to cool. Check the lids by pressing them with the finger. In case some of the jars with the quince jam are unsealed, place them into the fridge or reprocess the unsealed jars.

Nutritional Information (1 tbsp):

Calories: 45; Total fat: 1 oz; Total carbohydrates: 4 oz; Protein: 1 oz

# Plum Jam

---

*Prep Time: 40 min. | Makes: 5-6 11 oz jars*

---

Ingredients:

4.5 lb plums, pitted

3.5 cups of sugar

1 tsp. citric acid

1 tsp. cinnamon and cloves

2 tsp. pure orange extract

How to Prepare:

1. Halve the plums and boil them with the sugar over medium heat for 40 minutes, stirring all the time and removing the scum from the surface.

2. Spoon some jam on a plate and wait until thickened, if not continue boiling and testing every few minutes. The jam should be thick and gelled enough to spoon it into the jars. 5 minutes before the jam is ready mix in the citric acid, cinnamon, orange extract and cloves.

3. Remove the saucepan from the heat and spoon the freshly cooked jam into the sterilized jars up to 1/5 inch from the top and seal the jars.

4. Flip the jars upside down or boil for around 10 minutes and then leave to cool.

**Nutritional Information (1 tbsp):**

Calories: 53; Total fat: 2 oz; Total carbohydrates: 7 oz; Protein: 1 oz

# Baked Orange Plum Jam

---

*Prep Time: 2 hours│Makes: 6-7 11 oz jars*

---

## Ingredients:

5 lb plums, pitted and halved

2 tbsp. orange zest, minced

4 cups of sugar

2 tbsp. orange juice

1 tsp. cinnamon

## How to Prepare:

1. Combine the plums with the sugar and preheat the oven to 300°-360° Fahrenheit. Mix in some water, orange zest, orange juice and cinnamon and bake the plums for around 1.5-2 hours until thickened, if not continue baking. The jam should be gelled enough to spoon it into the jars.

2. Spoon the freshly baked jam into the sterilized jars up to 1/5 inch from the top and seal the jars.

3. Flip the jars upside down or boil for around 10 minutes and then leave to cool. Check the lids by pressing them with the finger. In case some of the jars with the orange and plum jam are unsealed, place them into the fridge or reprocess the unsealed jars.

## Nutritional Information (1 tbsp):

Calories: 58; Total fat: 2 oz; Total carbohydrates: 6 oz; Protein: 1 oz

# Apple Jam

*Prep Time: 40 min. | Makes: 3-4 10 oz jars*

Ingredients:

10 big apples, peeled and cubed

5 cups of sugar

1 tsp. Cinnamon

How to Prepare:

1. Boil the apples with the sugar over medium heat for around 40 minutes, stirring all the time.

2. Few minutes before the jam is ready stir in the cinnamon. Remove the saucepan from the heat and ladle freshly cooked jam into sterilized jars up to 1/5 inch from the top.

3. Seal the jars and then process them in a water bath. In a large pot, boil the jars for around 10 minutes and then take them out and leave to cool. Check the lids by pressing them with the finger. In case some of the jars with the apple jam are unsealed, place them into the fridge or reprocess the unsealed jam.

Nutritional Information (1 tbsp):

Calories: 50; Total fat: 1 oz; Total carbohydrates: 4 oz; Protein: 1 oz

# Plum Apple Jam

---

*Prep Time: 40 min.* | *Makes: 5-6 10 oz jars*

---

Ingredients:

2 cups of plums, pitted and halved

4 big and sweet Red Delicious or Fuji apples

4 cups of sugar

1.5 cups of water

1 tsp. Cinnamon

How to Prepare:

1. Boil the plums with the sugar and the water over medium heat for around 20 minutes, stirring all the time until the sugar dissolves. Remove the foam from the surface.

2. Add the apples and boil for 20 minutes more. The jam should be thick enough to spoon it into the jars. Few minutes before the jam is ready mix in the cinnamon.

3. When the jam is ready, remove the saucepan from the heat and ladle freshly cooked jam into sterilized jars up to 1/5 inch from the top.

4. Flip the jars upside down or boil for around 15 minutes and then leave to cool. Check the lids by pressing them with the finger. In case some of the jars with the plum and apple jam are unsealed, place them into the fridge or reprocess the unsealed jars.

Nutritional Information (1 tbsp):

Calories: 56; Total fat: 1 oz; Total carbohydrates: 4 oz; Protein: 1 oz

# Pear Apple Jam

*__Prep Time: 40 min.__ | __Makes: 4-5 10 oz jars__*

## Ingredients:

4 big pears, peeled and sliced

4 big apples, peeled and sliced

4 cups of sugar

1 cup of water

1 tsp. Cinnamon

1 tsp. citric acid

## How to Prepare:

1. Spoon the sugar over the fruits and set aside for few hours. Boil the pears and the apples with the sugar and the water over medium heat for around 40 minutes, stirring all the time until the sugar dissolves. Remove the foam from the surface.

2. The jam should be thick enough to spoon it into the jars. Few minutes before the jam is ready mix in the cinnamon and citric acid.

3. When the jam is ready, remove the saucepan from the heat and ladle freshly cooked jam into sterilized jars up to 1/5 inch from the top.

4. Seal the jars and then process them in a water bath. In a large pot, boil the jars for around 10 minutes and then take them out and leave to cool. Check the lids by pressing them with the finger. In case some of the jars are unsealed, place them into the fridge or reprocess the unsealed jars.

## Nutritional Information (1 tbsp):

Calories: 53; Total fat: 1 oz; Total carbohydrates: 4 oz; Protein: 1 oz

# Blackcurrant Apple Jam

---

*Prep Time: 30 min.* | *Makes: 4-5 11 oz jars*

---

## Ingredients:

3 lb blackcurrants

4 big apples, peeled and sliced

5 cups of sugar

1 tsp. Cinnamon

1 tsp. lemon juice

## How to Prepare:

1. Spoon the sugar over the fruits and set aside for few hours. Boil the blackcurrants and the apples with the sugar and some water over medium heat for around 30 minutes, stirring all the time until the sugar dissolves. Remove the foam from the surface.

2. The jam should be thick enough to spoon it into the jars. Few minutes before the jam is ready mix in the cinnamon and lemon juice.

3. When the jam is ready, remove the saucepan from the heat and ladle freshly cooked jam into sterilized jars up to 1/5 inch from the top.

4. Flip the jars upside down or boil for around 15 minutes and then leave to cool.

## Nutritional Information (1 tbsp):

Calories: 53; Total fat: 1 oz; Total carbohydrates: 4 oz; Protein: 1 oz

# Vanilla Pear Jam

---

*Prep Time: 30 min. | Makes: 4-5 11 oz jars*

---

Ingredients:

5 big pears, peeled and cubed

4 cups of sugar

½ cup of water

1 tsp. vanilla

1 tsp. citric acid

How to Prepare:

1. Boil the pears with the sugar, vanilla, citric acid and some water over medium heat for around 30 minutes, stirring all the time until the sugar dissolves. Remove the foam from the surface.

2. Spoon the freshly cooked jam into sterilized jars up to 1/5 inch from the top.

3. Seal the jars and then process them in a water bath. In a large pot, boil the jars for around 10 minutes and then take them out and leave to cool. Check the lids by pressing them with the finger. In case some of the jars with the vanilla and pear jam are unsealed, place them into the fridge or reprocess the unsealed jars.

Nutritional Information (1 tbsp):

Calories: 53; Total fat: 1 oz; Total carbohydrates: 4 oz; Protein: 2 oz

# Orange Pear Jam

---

***Prep Time: 30 min.*** | ***Makes: 4-5 11 oz jars***

---

## Ingredients:

5 big pears, peeled and cubed

4 cups of sugar

2 tbsp. orange zest, minced

½ cup of orange juice

1 tsp. vanilla

## How to Prepare:

1. Boil the pears with the sugar, vanilla, orange zest and orange juice over medium heat for around 30 minutes, stirring all the time until the sugar dissolves. Remove the foam from the surface.

2. Spoon the freshly cooked jam into sterilized jars up to 1/5 inch from the top.

3. Seal the jars and then process them in a water bath. In a large pot, boil the jars for around 10 minutes and then take them out and leave to cool. Check the lids by pressing them with the finger. In case some of the jars with the orange and pear jam are unsealed, place them into the fridge or reprocess the unsealed jars.

## Nutritional Information (1 tbsp):

Calories: 52; Total fat: 2 oz; Total carbohydrates: 5 oz; Protein: 1 oz

# Lemon Pear Jam

*Prep Time: 30 min. | Makes: 4-5 11 oz jars*

Ingredients:

5 big pears, peeled and cubed

4 cups of sugar

half cup of lemon juice

1 tsp. vanilla

1 tsp. lemon zest, minced

How to Prepare:

1. Boil the pears with the sugar, vanilla, lemon zest and lemon juice over medium heat for around 30 minutes, stirring all the time until the sugar dissolves. Remove the foam from the surface.

2. Spoon the freshly cooked jam into sterilized jars up to 1/5 inch from the top.

3. Seal the jars and then process them in a water bath. In a large pot, boil the jars for around 10 minutes and then take them out and leave to cool. Check the lids by pressing them with the finger. In case some of the jars with the lemon and pear jam are unsealed, place them into the fridge or reprocess the unsealed jars.

Nutritional Information (1 tbsp):

Calories: 53; Total fat: 1 oz; Total carbohydrates: 5 oz; Protein: 1 oz

# Almond Peach Jam

---

*Prep Time: 30 min.* | *Makes: 4-5 11 oz jars*

---

## Ingredients:

3 lb peaches, peeled and cubed

1 tbsp. pure almond extract

5 cups of sugar

1 tsp. citric acid

## How to Prepare:

1. Boil the peaches with the sugar over low heat for around 30 minutes, stirring all the time until the sugar dissolves. Remove the scum from the surface.

2. Pour some jam on a plate and check if it has gelled enough, by pressing with the finger, if not continue boiling and testing. The jam should be thick enough to spoon it into the jars. Few minutes before the jam is ready mix in the almond extract and citric acid.

3. When the jam is ready, remove the saucepan from the heat and ladle freshly cooked jam into the sterilized jars up to 1/5 inch from the top and seal the jars.

4. Seal the jars and then process them in a water bath. In a large pot, boil the jars for around 10 minutes and then take them out and leave to cool. Check the lids by pressing them with the finger. In case some of the jars with the peach jam are unsealed, place them into the fridge or reprocess the unsealed jars.

## Nutritional Information (1 tbsp):

Calories: 55; Total fat: 2 oz; Total carbohydrates: 5 oz; Protein: 2 oz

# Peach Jam

*Prep Time: 30 min.* | *Makes: 4-5 11 oz jars*

## Ingredients:

3 lb peaches, peeled and cubed

5 cups of sugar

2 tbsp. lime juice

## How to Prepare:

1. Boil the peaches with the sugar over low heat for around 30 minutes, stirring all the time until the sugar dissolves. Remove the scum from the surface.

2. Pour some jam on a plate and check if it has gelled enough, by pressing with the finger, if not continue boiling and testing. The jam should be thick enough to spoon it into the jars. Few minutes before the jam is ready stir in the lime juice.

3. When the jam is ready, remove the saucepan from the heat and ladle freshly cooked jam into the sterilized jars up to 1/5 inch from the top and seal the jars.

4. Seal the jars and then process them in a water bath. In a large pot, boil the jars for around 10 minutes and then take them out and leave to cool. Check the lids by pressing them with the finger. In case some of the jars with the peach jam are unsealed, place them into the fridge or reprocess the unsealed jars.

## Nutritional Information (1 tbsp):

Calories: 55; Total fat: 2 oz; Total carbohydrates: 6 oz; Protein: 1 oz

# Sugar-Free Cherry Jam

---

*Prep Time: 30 min.* | *Makes around 7 10 oz jars*

---

Ingredients:

8 cups of fresh cherries, washed and pitted

3 tbsp. granulated erythritol

2 tbsp. liquid stevia

2 tsp. citric acid

How to Prepare:

1. Boil the cherries with the erythritol over medium heat for around 30 minutes, stirring all the time until the erythritol dissolves. Skim the foam from the jam surface while boiling. Keep stirring until the cherry jam has thickened and gelled.

2. Add the stevia, and citric acid and remove the saucepan with the cherries from the heat and pour freshly cooked sugar-free cherry jam into the sterilized jars up to 1/4 inch from the top and seal the jars.

3. Then turn the jars upside down and leave them for overnight to cool completely and only then turn them back or process in the water bath. Check the lids by pressing them with the finger. In case some of the jars with the sugar-free cherry jam are unsealed, place them into the fridge or reprocess the unsealed jars.

Nutritional Information (1 tbsp):

Calories: 45; Total fat: 1 oz; Total carbohydrates: 4 oz; Protein: 1 oz

# Banana Cherry Jam

***Prep Time: 40 min.│Makes around 7 10 oz jars***

Ingredients:

5 lb fresh cherries, washed and pitted

1 banana, chopped

3 cups of white sugar

1 cup of brown sugar

0.5 oz pure banana extract

2 tsp. citric acid

2 tsp. vanilla

How to Prepare:

1.  Place the cherries and banana into a big saucepan and spoon the sugar on top and leave for at least few hours unrefrigerated at room temperature or place in the fridge for overnight.

2.  Then boil the cherries and banana mix over medium heat for around 10 minutes, stirring all the time until the sugar dissolves. Remove the foam from the surface. Then reduce the heat and continue to boil for around 30 minutes.

3.  Mix in the banana extract, citric acid, and vanilla and keep stirring until the cherries mixture has gelled and thickened. Pour some jam on a plate and check if gelled, pressing it with the finger, if not continue boiling and testing.

4.  Remove the saucepan with the cherries and banana jam from the heat and pour freshly cooked jam into sterilized and hot jars up to 1/5 inch from the top.

5.  Seal the jars and then turn the jars upside down. Leave them for overnight to cool completely and only then turn them back.

6. Or you can do it by processing the jars in the water bath and boiling them for around 10 minutes and then leaving to cool. It is important to remember to check the lids by pressing them with the finger. In case some of the jars with the banana cherry jam are unsealed, place them into the fridge or reprocess the unsealed jars.

Nutritional Information (1 tbsp):

Calories: 72; Total fat: 1 oz; Total carbohydrates: 6 oz; Protein: 1 oz

# Pineapple Cherry Jam

*Prep Time: 40 min.* | *Makes around 7 10 oz jars*

Ingredients:

7 cups of cherries

1 fresh and small pineapple, peeled and cut into rings

5 cups of sugar

2 tbsp. lemon juice

How to Prepare:

1. In a pot, combine the cherries and pineapple slices and spoon the sugar over the fruits, and then set aside for around four hours.

2. Boil the cherries with the pineapple slices over medium heat for around 40 minutes, stirring until the sugar dissolves. Remove the foam from the pineapple cherry jam.

3. Five minutes before the pineapple cherry jam is ready, stir in the lemon juice and keep stirring until the cherries and pineapple mixture has gelled enough. Continue

boiling and testing every five or ten minutes until the jam will get thick enough to spoon it into the jars.

4. Remove the saucepan with the cherries and pineapple slices from the heat and spoon freshly cooked jam into hot and sterilized jars up to 1/5 inch from the top.

5. Flip the jars with the pineapple cherry jam upside down or boil the jars in a large pot for around 10 minutes and then leave to cool. Check the lids by pressing them with the finger. In case some of the jars with the pineapple cherry jam are unsealed, place them into the fridge or reprocess the unsealed jars.

Nutritional Information (1 tbsp):

Calories: 51; Total fat: 2 oz; Total carbohydrates: 7 oz; Protein: 1 oz

# Banana Raspberry Jam

***Prep Time: 45 min. | Makes around 6 10 oz jars***

Ingredients:

8 cups of fresh raspberries

one banana, cubed

1 tsp. pure banana extract

5 cups of sugar

1 tsp. lemon juice

How to Prepare:

1. In a large pot, combine the raspberries with the banana and spoon the sugar over the fruits. Leave raspberries and banana for at least few hours unrefrigerated at room temperature or place the fruits into the fridge for 12 hours or overnight.

2. In the same pot boil the raspberries, banana, and sugar over medium heat for around 35-45 minutes, stirring all the time with a spoon until the sugar dissolves. Skim the foam from the raspberries jam. The best way to do that is to use a big spoon, dipper or ladle.

3. Few minutes before the jam is ready mix in the pure banana extract and lemon juice and keep stirring until the raspberries mixture has gelled. Pour one teaspoon of banana raspberry jam on a plate and wait until gelled, if not continue boiling and testing every 5 minutes. Remove the saucepan with the raspberries and banana from the heat and pour freshly cooked jam into sterilized jars up to 1/5 inch from the top to seal the hot jars.

4. Flip the jars upside down or boil for around 10 minutes and then leave to cool. Don't forget to check the lids by pressing them with the finger. In case some of the jars with the banana-raspberry jam are unsealed, place them into the fridge or reprocess the unsealed jars.

Nutritional Information (1 tbsp):
Calories: 67; Total fat: 0.9 oz; Total carbohydrates: 4 oz; Protein: 0.7 oz

# Pineapple Raspberry Jam

---

## *Prep Time: 40 min.│ Makes around 6 11 oz jars*

---

**Ingredients:**

8 cups of raspberries

1 can with crushed pineapples

5 cups of sugar

2 tbsp. lime juice

1 tsp. pure pineapple extract

**How to Prepare:**

1. In a large pot, boil the raspberries with the pineapples over medium heat for around 40 minutes, stirring until the sugar dissolves. Skim the foam from the pineapple raspberry jam.

2. Ten minutes before the pineapple raspberry jam is ready, mix in the lime juice and pure pineapple extract and keep stirring until the raspberries and pineapple mixture has gelled enough. Continue boiling and testing every five minutes until the jam gets thick enough to ladle it into the jars.

3. Remove the saucepan with the raspberries and pineapples from the heat and ladle freshly cooked jam into hot and sterilized jars up to 1/5 inch from the top.

4. Flip the jars with the pineapple raspberry jam upside down or boil for around 10 minutes and then leave to cool. Check the lids by pressing them with the finger. In case some of the jars with the pineapple raspberry jam are unsealed, place them into the fridge or reprocess the unsealed jars.

**Nutritional Information (1 tbsp):**

Calories: 48; Total fat: 2 oz; Total carbohydrates: 5 oz; Protein: 1 oz

# Almond Raspberry Jam

---

*Prep Time: 40 min. | Makes around 6 10 oz jars*

---

Ingredients:

8 cups of fresh raspberries, washed

1 tbsp. pure almonds extract

5 cups of sugar

1 tbsp. lemon juice

1 tsp. citric acid

**How to Prepare:**

1. In a large pot, combine the raspberries with the sugar. Leave the raspberries for at least few hours unrefrigerated at room temperature or place into the fridge for 10 hours or overnight.

2. Boil the raspberries, and sugar over medium heat for around 40 minutes, stirring all the time until the sugar dissolves. Remove the foam from the raspberries jam. The best way to do that is to use a big spoon or ladle.

3. 10 minutes before the jam is ready pour the pure almonds extract, lemon juice and citric acid and keep stirring until the raspberries mixture has gelled. Pour one teaspoon of raspberry jam on a plate and wait until gelled, pressing with the finger or the spoon. If not continue boiling and testing every 5-10 minutes.

4. Remove the saucepan with the raspberries from the heat and pour freshly cooked jam into sterilized jars up to 1/5 inch from the top to seal the hot jars.

5. Flip the jars upside down or boil them for around 10 minutes and then leave to cool. Don't forget to check the lids by pressing them with the finger. In case some of the jars with the almond raspberry jam are unsealed, place them into the fridge or reprocess the unsealed jars.

**Nutritional Information (1 tbsp):**

Calories: 64; Total fat: 1 oz; Total carbohydrates: 5 oz; Protein: 1 oz

# Sugar-Free Raspberry Jam

*Prep Time: 30 min. | Makes around 7 10 oz jars*

Ingredients:

5 lb fresh raspberries, washed

3 tbsp. granulated erythritol

1 tbsp. stevia

2 tbsp. lemon juice

How to Prepare:

1. Boil the raspberries mixture with the erythritol over medium heat for around 30 minutes, stirring all the time until erythritol dissolves. Remove the foam from the jam surface while boiling. Keep stirring until the raspberries jam has gelled.

2. Add the stevia, and lemon juice and remove the saucepan with the raspberries from the heat and pour freshly cooked sugar-free raspberry jam into the sterilized jars up to 1/4 inch from the top and seal the jars.

3. Then turn the jars upside down and leave them for overnight to cool completely and only then turn them back or process in the water bath. Check the lids by pressing them with the finger. In case some of the jars with the sugar-free raspberry jam are unsealed, place them into the fridge or reprocess the unsealed jars.

Nutritional Information (1 tbsp):

Calories: 45; Total fat: 1 oz; Total carbohydrates: 6 oz; Protein: 1 oz

# Village Strawberry Jam

---

*Prep Time: 30 min. │ Makes around 8 12 oz jars*

---

Ingredients:

5 lb fresh and big strawberries

6 cups of sugar

1 tsp. citric acid

1 tsp. cinnamon

How to Prepare:

1. In a saucepan, combine the sugar and the strawberries. Leave the strawberries for at least few hours unrefrigerated at room temperature.

2. Boil the strawberries over medium heat for around 30 minutes, stirring all the time with a spoon until the sugar dissolves but don't crush the berries. Skim the foam from the strawberry jam.

3. 5-10 min. before the jam is ready stir in the citric acid and cinnamon and keep stirring until the strawberries mixture has gelled enough. Spoon some jam on a plate and wait until thickened, if not continue boiling and testing every 5 minutes.

4. Remove the saucepan with the strawberries from the heat and ladle freshly cooked jam into sterilized jars up to 1/5 inch from the top.

5. Seal the jars and then flip the jars upside down. Leave them for overnight to cool completely and only then turn them back. Check the lids by pressing them with the finger. In case some of the jars with the strawberry jam are unsealed, place them into the fridge or reprocess the unsealed jars.

Nutritional Information (1 tbsp):

Calories: 59; Total fat: 2 oz; Total carbohydrates: 5.2 oz; Protein: 1.5 oz

# Lemon Strawberry Jam

---

*Prep Time: 30 min. | Makes around 7 12 oz jars*

---

Ingredients:

5 lb fresh, small strawberries

1 lemon, cut into rings

1 tsp. lemon zest, minced

6 cups of sugar

2 tbsp. lemon juice

How to Prepare:

1. In a saucepan, combine the strawberries and lemon slices and spoon the sugar over the fruits. Leave the strawberries for at least few hours unrefrigerated at room temperature.

2. Boil the strawberries and lemon slices over medium heat for around 30 minutes, stirring all the time with a spoon until the sugar dissolves but don't crush the berries or lemon slices. Remove the foam from the strawberry jam.

3. 10 min. before the jam is ready stir in the lemon zest and lemon juice and keep stirring until the strawberries and lemon mixture has gelled enough. Spoon some jam on a plate and wait until thickened, if not continue boiling and testing every 5 minutes.

4. Remove the saucepan with the strawberries from the heat and ladle freshly cooked jam into sterilized jars up to 1/5 inch from the top.

5. Flip the jars with the lemon strawberry jam upside down or boil for around 10 minutes and then leave to cool. Check the lids by pressing them with the finger. In case some of the jars with the lemon strawberry jam are unsealed, place them into the fridge or reprocess the unsealed jars.

Nutritional Information (1 tbsp):
Calories: 55; Total fat: 1 oz; Total carbohydrates: 5 oz; Protein: 1.2 oz

# Pineapple Strawberry Jam

---

*Prep Time: 40 min.* | *Makes around 7 10 oz jars*

---

**Ingredients:**

8 cups of small strawberries

1 fresh and small pineapple, peeled and cut into rings

6 cups of sugar

2 tbsp. orange juice

**How to Prepare:**

1. In a saucepan, combine the strawberries and pineapple slices and spoon the sugar over the fruits.

2. Boil the strawberries with the pineapple slices over medium heat for around 40 minutes, stirring until the sugar dissolves, but don't crush the berries nor pineapple slices. Skim the foam from the pineapple strawberry jam.

3. 5-10 minutes before the pineapple strawberry jam is ready, stir in the orange juice and keep stirring until the strawberries and pineapple mixture has gelled enough. Continue boiling and testing every 5 minutes until the jam will get thick enough to ladle it into the jars.

4. Remove the saucepan with the strawberries and pineapple slices from the heat and ladle freshly cooked jam into hot and sterilized jars up to 1/4 inch from the top.

5. Flip the jars with the pineapple strawberry jam upside down or boil for around 10 minutes and then leave to cool. Check the lids by pressing them with the finger. In case some of the jars with the pineapple strawberry jam are unsealed, place them into the fridge or reprocess the unsealed jars.

**Nutritional Information (1 tbsp):**

Calories: 50; Total fat: 1 oz; Total carbohydrates: 6 oz; Protein: 1 oz

# Banana Strawberry Jam

*Prep Time: 40 min.* | *Makes around 7 10 oz jars*

Ingredients:

5 lb small strawberries, washed

1 banana, chopped

4 cups of white sugar

0.5 oz pure banana extract

2 tsp. citric acid

2 tsp. vanilla

How to Prepare:

1. Place the strawberries and banana into a big saucepan and spoon the sugar over the fruits.

2. Boil the strawberries and banana mix over medium heat for around 40 minutes, stirring all the time until the sugar dissolves. Skim the foam from the surface.

3. Mix in the banana extract, citric acid, and vanilla and keep stirring until the strawberries mixture has gelled and thickened. Pour some jam on a plate and check if gelled, pressing it with the finger, if not continue boiling and testing.

4. Remove the saucepan with the strawberries and banana jam from the heat and pour freshly cooked jam into the hot jars up to 1/5 inch from the top.

5. Seal the jars and then turn them upside down. Leave the jars for overnight to cool completely and only then turn them back. Check the lids by pressing them with the finger. In case some of the jars are unsealed, place them into the fridge or reprocess the unsealed jars.

Nutritional Information (1 tbsp):

Calories: 63; Total fat: 2 oz; Total carbohydrates: 5 oz; Protein: 0.4 oz

# Apricot Jam

---

*Prep Time: 35 min.* | *Makes around 5 11 oz jars*

---

## Ingredients:

3 lb small apricots, cubed

4 cups of sugar

2 tsp. citric acid

## How to Prepare:

1. Wash and cube the apricots and place them into a big saucepan and then spoon the sugar over the apricots. Crack few stones and place the apricot kernels into the saucepan, this step will add specific flavors and an unforgettable taste to your apricot jam.

2. Boil the apricots over low heat for around 25-35 minutes, stirring all the time.

3. Mix in the citric acid and keep stirring until the apricots mixture has gelled. Put some jam on the plate and press down with your finger to check the density. Continue boiling and testing every five minutes until thickened.

4. Remove the saucepan with the apricot jam from the heat and carefully pour freshly cooked jam into the hot and sterilized jars up to 1/5 inch from the top.

5. Seal the jars and then turn them upside down or boil for around 10 minutes and then leave to cool. Check the lids by pressing them with the finger. In case some of the jars with the apricot jam are unsealed, place them into the fridge or reprocess the unsealed jars.

## Nutritional Information (1 tbsp):

Calories: 62; Total fat: 1 oz; Total carbohydrates: 7 oz; Protein: 0.6 oz

# Grandma's Apricot Jam

**Prep Time: 35 min. | Makes around 5 11 oz jars**

Ingredients:

6 cups of apricots, chopped

4 cups of sugar

2 tsp. lemon juice

2 tsp. vanilla

How to Prepare:

1. Wash and chop the apricots and place them into the pot and then mix in the sugar. Leave the apricots for at least few hours unrefrigerated at room temperature.

2. Boil the apricots over medium heat for around 30 minutes, stirring all the time until the sugar dissolves. Remember to remove the scum from the surface.

3. Mix in the lemon juice and vanilla and keep stirring until the apricots mixture has gelled. Put some apricot jam on the plate and press down with your finger to check the density. Continue boiling and testing every five or ten minutes until thickened enough to spoon it into the jars.

4. Remove the pot with the apricot jam from the heat and carefully spoon freshly cooked jam into the hot and sterilized jars up to 1/5 inch from the top.

5. Seal the jars and then turn them upside down or boil for around 10 minutes and then leave to cool. Check the lids by pressing them with the finger. In case some of the jars with the apricot jam are unsealed, place them into the fridge or reprocess the unsealed jars.

**Nutritional Information (1 tbsp):**

Calories: 60; Total fat: 1 oz; Total carbohydrates: 5 oz; Protein: 0.5 oz

# Orange Apricot Jelly

*Prep Time: 50 min.* | *Makes around 5 10 oz jars*

Ingredients:

3 lb apricots, cubed

4 cups of sugar

2 cups of orange juice

2 tbsp. orange zest, minced

2 tsp. citric acid

How to Prepare:

1. Place the apricots into a big saucepan and then boil them with the water for around 15-20 minutes. Then strain the apricots to get 4-5 cups of the juice.

2. In a saucepan, combine the apricot juice with the sugar, orange juice, orange zest, and citric acid and boil the juice for 30 minutes until the sugar dissolves. Remove the foam from the surface. Pour some jelly on the plate to check the density. Continue boiling and testing every five minutes until thickened.

3. Remove the saucepan from the heat and ladle the freshly cooked jelly into the sterilized jars and seal the jars.

4. Flip the jars upside down or boil for around 10 minutes and then leave to cool. In case some of the jars with the orange apricot jelly are unsealed, place them into the fridge or reprocess the unsealed jars.

Nutritional Information (1 tbsp):

Calories: 49; Total fat: 1 oz; Total carbohydrates: 6 oz; Protein: 1 oz

# Lemon Apricot Jelly

---

### *Prep Time: 50 min.│Makes around 5 10 oz jars*

---

Ingredients:

3 lb apricots, cubed

4 cups of sugar

1 cup of lemon juice

1 tbsp. lemon zest, minced


How to Prepare:

1. Place the apricots into a big saucepan and then boil them with the water for around 15-20 minutes. Then strain the apricots to get 4-5 cups of the juice.

2. In a saucepan, combine the apricot juice with the sugar, lemon juice, and lemon zest and boil the juice for 30 minutes until the sugar dissolves. Remove the foam from the surface. Pour some jelly on the plate to check the density. Continue boiling and testing every five minutes until thickened.

3. Remove the saucepan from the heat and ladle the freshly cooked jelly into the sterilized jars and seal the jars.

4. Flip the jars upside down or boil for around 10 minutes and then leave to cool. In case some of the jars with the lemon apricot jelly are unsealed, place them into the fridge or reprocess the unsealed jars.


Nutritional Information (1 tbsp):

Calories: 47; Total fat: 2 oz; Total carbohydrates: 7 oz; Protein: 1 oz

# Orange Pumpkin Jam

*Prep Time: 50 min.* | *Makes around 8 10 oz jars*

Ingredients:

3 lb pumpkin, peeled and cubed

1 orange, peeled and sliced

4 cups of sugar

1 cup of raisins

2 tbsp. orange zest, minced

How to Prepare:

1. Place the pumpkin into a big saucepan and spoon the sugar on top and leave for at least few hours unrefrigerated at room temperature or place in the fridge overnight.

2. In a saucepan, combine the pumpkin, orange, orange zest and raisins and simmer the pumpkin mixture for 50 minutes until the sugar dissolves and pumpkin is soft. Remove the foam from the surface.

3. Spoon the freshly cooked pumpkin jam into the sterilized and hot jars and seal the jars.

4. Flip the jars upside down or boil for around 10 minutes and then leave to cool. In case some of the jars with the orange pumpkin jam are unsealed, place them into the fridge or reprocess the unsealed jars.

Nutritional Information (1 tbsp):

Calories: 59; Total fat: 2 oz; Total carbohydrates: 6 oz; Protein: 1 oz

# Pears Pumpkin Jam

---

*Prep Time: 40 min.│Makes around 8 11 oz jars*

---

Ingredients:

2 lb pumpkin, peeled and cubed

2 pears, peeled and cubed

1 sour apple, peeled and cubed

4 cups of sugar

1/3 cup of apple juice

½ tsp. cinnamon

How to Prepare:

1. Place the cubed pumpkin, pears and apple into a large pot and spoon the sugar on top and leave for at least few hours unrefrigerated at room temperature or place in the fridge overnight.

2. In a pot, combine the pumpkin, pears, apple, and apple juice and then boil the pumpkin mixture for around 40 minutes on medium heat, stirring until the sugar dissolves. Pumpkin should be soft. Remember to remove the foam from the surface. Few minutes before the jam is ready stir in the cinnamon. The pears pumpkin jam should be gelled enough to ladle it into the jars.

3. Ladle the freshly cooked pears pumpkin jam into the sterilized and hot jars and seal the jars.

4. Flip the jars upside down or boil for around 10 minutes and then leave to cool. In case some of the jars with the pears pumpkin jam are unsealed, place them into the fridge or reprocess the unsealed jars.

Nutritional Information (1 tbsp):

Calories: 55; Total fat: 1 oz; Total carbohydrates: 7 oz; Protein: 2 oz

# Grandma's Pumpkin Jam

*Prep Time: 45 min. | Makes around 6 10 oz jars*

Ingredients:

2 lb pumpkin, peeled and cubed

3 cups of sugar

1 cup of brown

3 tbsp. lemon juice

2 tsp. citric acid

1 tsp. vanilla

How to Prepare:

1. Spoon the white sugar over the cubed pumpkin and leave for at least few hours unrefrigerated at room temperature or place in the fridge overnight.

2. In a pot, boil the pumpkin for around 45 minutes on medium heat, stirring until the sugar dissolves. Stir in the brown sugar. Pumpkin should be soft. Remember to

remove the foam from the surface. Five minutes before the pumpkin jam is ready mix in the citric acid, lemon juice, and vanilla. The pumpkin jam should be gelled enough to ladle it into the jars.

3. Ladle the freshly boiled pumpkin jam into the sterilized and hot jars and seal the jars.

4. Flip the jars upside down or boil for around 10 minutes and then leave to cool. In case some of the jars with the pumpkin jam are unsealed, place them into the fridge or reprocess the unsealed jars.

Nutritional Information (1 tbsp):

Calories: 51; Total fat: 2 oz; Total carbohydrates: 6 oz; Protein: 1 oz

# Banana Gooseberry Jam

*Prep Time: 40 min.* │ *Makes around 6 11 oz jars*

Ingredients:

5 cups of gooseberries

2 bananas, sliced

1 tsp. pure banana extract

5 cups of sugar

3 tbsp. lemon juice, freshly squeezed

How to Prepare:

1. Wash the gooseberries and then spoon the sugar over the berries and bananas and leave for few hours unrefrigerated at room temperature.

2. In a large pot, boil the gooseberries and bananas with the sugar over medium heat for around 40 minutes, stirring all the time until the sugar dissolves. Keep removing the foam and scum constantly.

3. Five minutes before the jam is ready mix in the lemon juice and pure banana extract and keep stirring until the gooseberries and banana mixture has thickened and gelled.

4. When the jam is ready, spoon the freshly cooked banana gooseberry jam into the hot and sterilized jars.

5. Seal the jars and then process them in a water bath. In a large pot, boil the jars for around 10 minutes and then take them out and leave to cool. Check the lids by pressing them with the finger. In case some of the jars with the banana gooseberry jam are unsealed, place them into the fridge or reprocess the unsealed jars.

Nutritional Information (1 tbsp):

Calories: 65; Total fat: 2 oz; Total carbohydrates: 5.1 oz; Protein: 0.7 oz

# Pineapple Gooseberry Jam

---

***Prep Time: 40 min.| Makes around 7 10 oz jars***

---

Ingredients:

6 cups of gooseberries

1 fresh and small pineapple, peeled and cut into rings

1 tsp. pure pineapple extract

5 cups of brown sugar

2 tbsp. lemon juice

How to Prepare:

1. In a saucepan, combine the gooseberries and pineapple slices and spoon the sugar over the fruits.

2. Boil the gooseberries with the pineapple slices over medium heat for around 40 minutes, stirring until the sugar dissolves, but don't crush the berries nor pineapple slices. Remove the foam and the scum from the pineapple gooseberry jam surface.

3. Five or ten minutes before the pineapple gooseberry jam is ready, stir in the lemon juice and pure pineapple extract. Keep stirring until the pineapple and gooseberries mixture has gelled enough. Continue boiling and testing every five or ten minutes until the jam will get thick enough to ladle it into the jars.

4. Remove the saucepan with the pineapple gooseberry jam from the heat and ladle freshly cooked jam into hot and sterilized jars up to 1/4 inch from the top.

5. Flip the jars with the pineapple gooseberry jam upside down or boil for around 10 minutes and then leave to cool. Check the lids by pressing them with the finger. In case some of the jars with the pineapple gooseberry jam are unsealed, place them into the fridge or reprocess the unsealed jars.

Nutritional Information (1 tbsp):

Calories: 51; Total fat: 1 oz; Total carbohydrates: 7 oz; Protein: 2 oz

# Pineapple Blueberry Jam

*Prep Time: 40 min.* | *Makes around 6 10 oz jars*

Ingredients:

5 cups of blueberries, fresh

5 cups of sugar

2 tbsp. pure pineapple extract

2 tsp. citric acid

How to Prepare:

1. Pour the sugar over the blueberries and set aside at room temperature for at least few hours or place the blueberries in the fridge overnight.

2. In a big saucepan, boil the blueberries over medium heat for around 40 minutes, stirring all the time with a spoon until the sugar dissolves. Remove the foam from the blueberry jam surface.

3. Few minutes before the jam is ready mix in the pure pineapple extract and citric acid and keep stirring until the blueberries jam has gelled. Spoon some pineapple blueberry jam on a plate and wait until thickened, if not continue boiling and testing until thickened and gelled.

4. When the jam is ready, remove the saucepan with the blueberries from the heat and pour freshly cooked jam into the hot and sterilized jars up to 1/5 inch from the top.

5. Seal the jars with the pineapple blueberry jam and flip them upside down or boil them for around 10 minutes and then leave to cool. Check the lids by pressing them with the finger. In case some of the jars with the pineapple blueberry jam are unsealed, place them into the fridge or reprocess the unsealed jars.

Nutritional Information (1 tbsp):

Calories: 60; Total fat: 0.2 oz; Total carbohydrates: 5 oz; Protein: 1 oz

# Baked Lemon Plum Jam

*Prep Time: 2 hours | Makes around 7 11 oz jars*

Ingredients:

8 cups of plums, stoned and halved

2 tbsp. lemon zest, minced

5 cups of sugar

half cup of lemon juice

1 tsp. vanilla

baking spray or unsalted butter

How to Prepare:

1. Combine the plums with the sugar and preheat the oven to 320°-340° Fahrenheit and then coat the baking pan with the baking spray or unsalted butter.

2. Pour half cup of water and half cup of lemon juice. Then stir in the lemon zest, and vanilla and bake the plums for around 2 hours until gelled and thickened, if not

continue baking and testing every five to ten minutes. The lemon plum jam should be gelled enough to ladle it into the jars.

3. When the lemon plum jam is ready ladle the freshly baked jam into the sterilized and hot jars up to 1/4 inch from the top and then seal the jars.

4. Flip the jars upside down or boil for around 10 minutes and then leave to cool. Check the lids by pressing them with the finger. In case some of the jars with the lemon and plum jam are unsealed, place them into the fridge or reprocess the unsealed jars.

Nutritional Information (1 tbsp):

Calories: 56; Total fat: 1 oz; Total carbohydrates: 6 oz; Protein: 1 oz

# Cherry Jam with Bananas

*__Prep Time: 40 min.__* | *__Makes around 10 10 oz jars__*

Ingredients:

6 lb fresh cherries, washed and pitted

1.5 lb bananas, chopped

3 cups of white sugar

1 cup of brown sugar

2 tsp. pure banana extract

2 tsp. citric acid

2 tsp. vanilla

How to Prepare:

1. Place the cherries and bananas into a big saucepan and spoon the sugar on top. Leave for at least few hours unrefrigerated at room temperature or place in the fridge overnight. Mash the cherries and bananas using a potato masher.

2. Then boil the cherries and bananas mix over the medium heat for around 10 minutes, stirring all the time until the sugar dissolves. Remove the foam from the surface. Then reduce the heat and continue to boil for around 30 minutes.

3. Mix in the banana extract, citric acid, and vanilla and keep stirring until the cherries mixture has gelled and thickened. Pour some jam on a plate and check if gelled, pressing it with the finger, if not continue boiling and testing.

4. Remove the saucepan with the cherries and banana jam from the heat and pour the freshly cooked jam into sterilized and hot jars up to 1/5 inch from the top.

5. Seal the jars and then turn the jars upside down. Leave them for overnight to cool completely and only then turn them back.

6. Or you can do it by processing the jars in the water bath and boiling them for around 10 minutes and then leaving to cool. It is important to remember to check the lids by pressing them with the finger. In case some of the jars with the banana cherry jam are unsealed, place them into the fridge or reprocess the unsealed jars.

**Nutritional Information (1 tbsp):**

Calories: 72; Total fat: 6 oz; Total carbohydrates: 10 oz; Protein: 5 oz

# Mango & Cherry Jam

---

### *Prep Time: 40 min.* | *Makes around 6 10 oz jars*

---

Ingredients:

7 cups of cherries

2 mangos, peeled and diced

5 cups of sugar

2 tbsp. lemon juice

How to Prepare:

1. In a pot, combine the cherries and mangos and spoon the sugar over the fruits, and then set aside for around 4 hours.

2. Boil the cherries with the mango cubes over medium heat for around 40 minutes, stirring until the sugar dissolves. Remove the foam from the jam.

3. Five minutes before the cherry jam is ready, stir in the lemon juice and keep stirring until the cherries and mangos mixture has gelled enough. Continue boiling and testing every five or ten minutes until the jam will get thick enough to spoon it into the jars.

4. Remove the saucepan with the cherries and mangos from the heat and spoon freshly cooked jam into hot and sterilized jars up to 1/5 inch from the top.

5. Flip the jars with the mango-cherry jam upside down or boil the jars in a large pot for around 10 minutes and then leave to cool. Check the lids by pressing them with the finger. In case some of the jars with the jam are unsealed, place them into the fridge or reprocess the unsealed jars.

Nutritional Information (1 tbsp):

Calories: 51; Total fat: 2 oz; Total carbohydrates: 8 oz; Protein: 3 oz

# Vanilla Taste Blackcurrant Jelly

*Prep Time: 50 min. | Makes: 6-7 11 oz jars*

## Ingredients:

6 cups of blackcurrants, fresh

5 cups of sugar

3 tbsp. pure vanilla extract

## How to Prepare:

1. Spoon 4 tbsp. sugar over the blackcurrants and set aside for few hours and then mash the berries using the potato masher.

2. Pour some water and boil the blackcurrants over the low heat for around 15-20 minutes, stirring all the time. Then strain the blackcurrants to get 4 cups of the juice.

3. In a saucepan, combine the juice with the sugar and boil the juice for 30 minutes. The jelly should be thick enough to ladle it into the jars. If not, add more sugar. Remove the foam from the surface.

4. Remove the saucepan from the heat and ladle the freshly cooked jelly into the sterilized jars and seal the jars.

5. Flip the jars upside down or boil for around 10 minutes and then leave to cool. Check the lids by pressing them with the finger. In case some of the jars with the blackcurrant jelly are unsealed, place them into the fridge or reprocess the unsealed jars.

## Nutritional Information (1 tbsp):

Calories: 54; Total fat: 2 oz; Total carbohydrates: 7 oz; Protein: 3 oz

# Vanilla-Almond Raspberry Jam

---

### *Prep Time: 40 min.│Makes around 7 10 oz jars*

---

Ingredients:

8 cups of fresh raspberries, washed

1 tbsp. pure almonds extract

1 tbsp. pure vanilla extract

5 cups of sugar

1 tbsp. lemon juice

1 tsp. citric acid

How to Prepare:

1. In a large pot, combine the raspberries with the sugar. Leave the raspberries for at least few hours unrefrigerated at room temperature or place into the fridge for 10 hours or overnight.

2. Boil the raspberries, and sugar over medium heat for around 40 minutes, stirring all the time until the sugar dissolves. Remove the foam from the raspberries jam. The best way to do that is to use a big spoon or ladle.

3. 10 minutes before the jam is ready pour the pure almonds extract, vanilla extract, lemon juice and citric acid and keep stirring until the raspberries mixture has gelled. Pour one teaspoon of raspberry jam on a plate and wait until gelled, pressing with the finger or the spoon. If not continue boiling and testing every 5-10 minutes.

4. Remove the saucepan with the raspberries from the heat and pour freshly cooked jam into sterilized jars up to 1/5 inch from the top to seal the hot jars.

5. Flip the jars upside down or boil them for around 10 minutes and then leave to cool. Don't forget to check the lids by pressing them with the finger. In case some of the jars with the almond raspberry jam are unsealed, place them into the fridge or reprocess the unsealed jars.

Nutritional Information (1 tbsp):
Calories: 64; Total fat: 5 oz; Total carbohydrates: 10 oz; Protein: 2 oz

*Prep Time: 30 min.* | *Makes around 7 12 oz jars*

Ingredients:

5 lb fresh blueberries, washed

4 tbsp. granulated erythritol

3 tbsp. stevia

2 tbsp. lemon juice

How to Prepare:

1. Boil the blueberries mixture with the erythritol over medium heat for around 30 minutes, stirring all the time until erythritol dissolves. Remove the foam from the jam surface while boiling. Keep stirring until the blueberries jam has gelled.

2. Add the stevia and lemon juice and remove the saucepan with the blueberries from the heat and pour the freshly cooked sugar-free blueberry jam into the sterilized jars up to 1/4 inch from the top and seal the jars.

3. Then turn the jars upside down and leave them for overnight to cool completely and only then turn them back or process in the water bath. Check the lids by pressing them with the finger. In case some of the jars with the sugar-free blueberries jam are unsealed, place them into the fridge or reprocess the unsealed jars.

Nutritional Information (1 tbsp):

Calories: 45; Total fat: 4 oz; Total carbohydrates: 8 oz; Protein: 3 oz

# Almond Strawberry Jam

---

*Prep Time: 40 min.│ Makes around 8 10 oz jars*

---

Ingredients:

9 cups of fresh and sweet strawberries

4 cups of white sugar

1 cup of brown sugar

2 tsp. pure almond extract

1 tsp. vanilla

How to Prepare:

1.  Place the strawberries into a big saucepan and spoon the white sugar on top.

2.  In the same saucepan boil the strawberries mixture with the brown sugar over medium heat for around 40 minutes, stirring all the time until sugar dissolves. Skim the foam from the strawberries jam. Keep stirring until the strawberries jam has thickened and gelled enough. Add in the pure almond extract and vanilla.

3.  Remove the saucepan with the strawberries from the heat and pour freshly cooked jam into hot jars up to 1/4 inch from the top.

4. Seal the jars and then process them in the water bath. In a large pot, boil the jars for around 10 minutes and then take them out and leave to cool. Check the lids by pressing them with the finger. In case some of the jars with the almond strawberry jam are unsealed, place them into the fridge or reprocess the unsealed jars.

Nutritional Information (1 tbsp):

Calories: 49; Total fat: 1 oz; Total carbohydrates: 4 oz; Protein: 2 oz

# Peanuts Gooseberry Jam

---

*Prep Time: 50 min.│ Makes: 7-8 10 oz jars*

---

Ingredients:

2 lb gooseberries

1 cup of peanuts

4 cups of brown sugar

3 tbsp. lemon juice, squeezed

2 tsp. vanilla


How to Prepare:

1. Grind the peanuts. In a bowl, combine the sugar with the vanilla and mix well.

2. Then place the gooseberries into a big saucepan and spoon the sugar-vanilla mixture on top and leave for at least 6 hours unrefrigerated at room temperature or place in the fridge overnight.

3. In the same saucepan boil the gooseberries and sugar-vanilla mixture over high heat for around 10 minutes, stirring all the time with a spoon until sugar dissolves.

4. Then reduce the heat and continue to boil for around 40 minutes but don't forget to skim the foam from the berries.

5. Pour the lemon juice and keep stirring until the berries mixture has gelled and thickened.

6. Remove the saucepan with the gooseberries from the heat and pour the freshly cooked jam into the sterilized jars up to 1/5 inch from the top.

7. Seal the jars and then turn the jars upside down. Leave them for overnight to cool completely and only then turn them back.

Nutritional Information (1 tbsp):

Calories: 67; Total fat: 1 oz; Total carbohydrates: 4 oz; Protein: 0.8 oz

# Grandma's Strawberry Jam

**_Prep Time: 40 min._** | **_Makes: 5-6 10 oz jars_**

Ingredients:

3 lb small and sweet strawberries

2 cups of brown sugar

2 cups of white, table sugar

3 tbsp. lemon juice, squeezed

1 tsp. vanilla

How to Prepare:

1. In a bowl, combine the brown sugar and white sugar with vanilla and mix well.

2. Then spoon the strawberries into a big saucepan and add the sugar-vanilla mixture on top. Leave the berries for at least 2 hours unrefrigerated at room temperature.

3. In the same saucepan boil the raspberries and sugar-vanilla mixture over the high heat for around 10 minutes, stirring all the time with a spoon until sugar dissolves.

4. Then reduce the heat and continue to boil for around 30 minutes but don't forget to skim the foam from the berries.

5. Pour the lemon juice and keep stirring until the strawberries mixture has thickened.

6. Remove the saucepan with the strawberries from the heat and pour the freshly cooked jam into the sterilized jars up to 1/5 inch from the top.

7. Seal the jars and then turn the jars upside down. Leave them for overnight to cool completely and only then turn them back.

8. Or you can do it more traditionally by placing the jars into the water bath and boiling for around 7-10 minutes and then leaving to cool. Check the lids by pressing them with the finger. In case some of the jars with the raspberry jam are unsealed, place them into the fridge or reprocess the unsealed jars.

Nutritional Information (1 tbsp):

Calories: 60; Total fat: 2 oz; Total carbohydrates: 4 oz; Protein: 0.8 oz

# Kiwi Blackcurrant Jam

*__Prep Time: 40 min.__* │ *__Makes: 6-7 11 oz jars__*

## Ingredients:

2.5 lbs blackcurrants

2 lbs kiwi's, peeled and diced

5 cups of sugar

2 tbsp. orange juice

## How to Prepare:

1. Boil the blackcurrants with the kiwi's and sugar over medium heat for around 40 minutes, stirring all the time and removing the foam from the surface.

2. Spoon some jam on a plate and wait until thickened, if not continue boiling and testing until gelled. The jam should be thick enough to ladle it into the jars. 10 minutes before the jam is ready mix in the orange zest and orange juice.

3. Remove the saucepan from the heat and ladle freshly cooked jam into sterilized jars up to 1/5 inch from the top and seal the jars.

4. Flip the jars with the jam upside down or boil for around 10 minutes and then leave to cool. In case some of the jars with the blackcurrant jam are unsealed, place them into the fridge or reprocess the unsealed jars.

## Nutritional Information (1 tbsp):

Calories: 53; Total fat: 5 oz; Total carbohydrates: 9 oz; Protein: 2 oz

# Lemon-Strawberry Jam

*Prep Time: 50 min.* | *Makes: 7-8 10 oz jars*

Ingredients:

5 lb fresh and sweet strawberries

2 lemons, diced

5 cups of sugar

1 tbsp. citric acid

1 tsp. vanilla

How to Prepare:

1. Spoon 2 cups of the sugar over the diced lemons. Leave them for at least 3 hours unrefrigerated at room temperature or place in the fridge overnight.
2. Place the strawberries into a big saucepan and boil with the remaining sugar and lemons.
3. Boil the strawberries mixture over medium heat for around 30 minutes, stirring all the time until the sugar dissolves. Remove the foam from the strawberries jam while boiling. Keep stirring until the strawberries jam has gelled.
4. Remove the saucepan with the strawberries from the heat and pour freshly cooked jam into sterilized jars up to 1/5 inch from the top.
5. Seal the jars and then turn the jars upside down. Leave them for overnight to cool completely and only then turn them back. Check the lids by pressing them with the finger. In case some of the jars with the strawberry jam are unsealed, place them into the fridge or reprocess the unsealed jars.

Nutritional Information (1 tbsp):

Calories: 50; Total fat: 4 oz; Total carbohydrates: 3 oz; Protein: 2 oz

# Orange Taste Gooseberry Jam

***Prep Time: 40 min.*** | ***Makes: 5-6 11 oz jars***

## Ingredients:

4 cups of gooseberries

2 tbsp. orange zest, minced

5 cups of brown sugar

3 tbsp. orange juice, freshly squeezed

## How to Prepare:

1. Wash the gooseberries and then stir in the brown sugar and leave for at least 2 hours unrefrigerated at room temperature.

2. In a large saucepan, boil the gooseberries with the sugar over medium heat for around 30-40 minutes, stirring all the time until the sugar dissolves and removing the foam.

3. Few minutes before the jam is ready mix in the orange juice and orange zest and keep stirring until the gooseberries mixture has thickened and gelled.

4. When the jam is ready, ladle freshly cooked gooseberries jam into the sterilized jars.

5. Seal the jars and then process them in a water bath. In a large pot, boil the jars for around 10 minutes and then take them out and leave to cool. Check the lids by pressing them with the finger. In case some of the jars with the orange and gooseberry jam are unsealed, place them into the fridge or reprocess the unsealed jars.

## Nutritional Information (1 tbsp):

Calories: 62; Total fat: 4 oz; Total carbohydrates: 7.3 oz; Protein: 3 oz

# Cherry Jelly

*Prep Time: 1 hour | Makes: 6-7 11 oz jars*

Ingredients:

2 lbs cherries, pitted

5 cups of sugar

2 tsp. citric acid

How to Prepare:

1. Spoon 1 cup of sugar over the berries and set aside for overnight.

2. Boil the berries over the low heat for around 30 minutes, stirring all the time. Then mash the berries with the potato masher and strain the mixture to get 4-5 cups of the juice.

3. In a saucepan, combine the juice with the remaining sugar and boil the juice for 30 minutes until thickened. The jelly should be thick enough to pour it into the jars. Skim the foam from the surface. 10 minutes before the jelly is ready mix in the citric acid.

4. Remove the saucepan from the heat and pour the freshly cooked jelly into the sterilized jars.

5. Turn the jars upside down or boil for around 10 minutes and then leave to cool. Check the lids by pressing them with the finger. In case some of the jars with the cherry jelly are unsealed, place them into the fridge or reprocess the unsealed jars.

Nutritional Information (1 tbsp):

Calories: 57; Total fat: 4 oz; Total carbohydrates: 8 oz; Protein: 3 oz

# Sugar-Free Orange Strawberry Jam

---

*Prep Time: 40 min.* | *Makes: 6-7 11 oz jars*

---

**Ingredients:**

4 lb fresh and small strawberries

2 oranges, peeled and diced

2 tbsp. orange zest, minced

3 tbsp. erythritol, granulated

2 tbsp. orange juice, freshly squeezed


**How to Prepare:**

1.  In a saucepan, combine the erythritol and 1 cup of water and boil the mixture until the erythritol dissolves.

2.  Add the strawberries and oranges. Boil over medium heat for around 40 minutes, stirring all the time with a spoon until the sugar dissolves. Don't forget to skim the foam from the strawberry jam.

3.  5-7 min. before the jam is ready mix in the orange juice and orange zest and keep stirring until the strawberries mixture has thickened. Spoon some jam on a plate and wait until thickened, if not continue boiling and testing.

4.  When the jam is ready, remove the saucepan with the strawberries from the heat and spoon freshly cooked jam into sterilized jars up to 1/5 inch from the top.

5.  Seal the jars and then turn the jars upside down. Leave them for overnight to cool completely and only then turn them back. Check the lids by pressing them with the finger. In case some of the jars are unsealed, place them into the fridge or reprocess the unsealed jars.


**Nutritional Information (1 tbsp):**

Calories: 65; Total fat: 1.3 oz; Total carbohydrates: 5 oz; Protein: 2 oz

# Gooseberry and Raspberry Jam

---

*Prep Time: 40 min.│ Makes: 5-6 11 oz jars*

---

Ingredients:

1.5 lb gooseberries

1.5 lb raspberries

5 cups of sugar

1 tbsp. lemon juice or half tsp. citric acid

How to Prepare:

1. In a big pot, combine berries with the sugar and leave for 2 hours unrefrigerated at room temperature.

2. Boil the berries with the sugar for 40 minutes, stirring until the sugar dissolves and removing the foam and scum from the surface.

3. 5 minutes before the jam is ready mix in the lemon juice or citric acid and keep stirring until the berries jam has thickened.

4. Ladle freshly cooked berries jam into sterilized jars up to 1/4 inch from the top and then seal the jars.

5. Now turn the jars upside down and leave them for at least 5 hours or for overnight to cool completely and only then turn them back. Check the lids by pressing them with the finger. In case some of the jars with the gooseberry jam are unsealed, place them into the fridge or reprocess the unsealed jars.

Nutritional Information (1 tbsp):

Calories: 64; Total fat: 3 oz; Total carbohydrates: 7 oz; Protein: 4 oz

# Blueberry Jelly

*Prep Time: 1 hour | Makes: 6-7 11 oz jars*

Ingredients:

3 lbs blueberries

5 cups of sugar

2 tsp. citric acid

How to Prepare:

1. Spoon 1 cup of the sugar over the berries and set aside for overnight.

2. Boil the blueberries over the low heat for around 30 minutes, stirring all the time. Pour in some water. Then mash the blueberries with the potato masher and strain the mixture to get 4-5 cups of the juice.

3. In a saucepan, combine the juice with the remaining sugar and boil the juice for 30 minutes until thickened. The jelly should be thick enough to pour it into the jars. Skim the foam from the surface. 10 minutes before the jelly is ready mix in the citric acid.

4. Remove the saucepan from the heat and pour the freshly cooked jelly into the sterilized jars.

5. Turn the jars upside down or boil for around 10 minutes and then leave to cool. Check the lids by pressing them with the finger. In case some of the jars with the blueberry jelly are unsealed, place them into the fridge or reprocess the unsealed jars.

Nutritional Information (1 tbsp):

Calories: 57; Total fat: 4 oz; Total carbohydrates: 8 oz; Protein: 3 oz

# Blackcurrant & Redcurrant Jelly

*Prep Time: 1 hour* | *Makes: 6-7 11 oz jars*

Ingredients:

2 cups of blackcurrants

2 cups of redcurrants

5 cups of sugar

2 tsp. citric acid

How to Prepare:

1. Spoon 1 cup of sugar over the berries and set aside for overnight.

2. Pour 5 cups of water and boil the berries with the over low heat for around 30 minutes, stirring all the time. Then mash the berries with the potato masher and strain the mixture to get 4-5 cups of the juice.

3. In a saucepan, combine the juice with the remaining sugar and boil the juice for 30 minutes until thickened. The jelly should be thick enough to pour it into the jars. Skim the foam from the surface. 10 minutes before the jelly is ready mix in the citric acid.

4. Remove the saucepan from the heat and pour the freshly cooked jelly into the sterilized jars.

5. Turn the jars upside down or boil for around 10 minutes and then leave to cool. Check the lids by pressing them with the finger. In case some of the jars with the redcurrant jelly are unsealed, place them into the fridge or reprocess the unsealed jars.

Nutritional Information (1 tbsp):

Calories: 57; Total fat: 5 oz; Total carbohydrates: 10 oz; Protein: 3 oz

# Apples & Blackcurrant Jam

---

*Prep Time: 40 min.*│*Makes: 6-7 11 oz jars*

---

Ingredients:

2.5 lbs blackcurrants

2 lbs apples, peeled and diced

5 cups of sugar

2 tbsp. orange juice

How to Prepare:

1. Boil the blackcurrants with the apples and sugar over medium heat for around 40 minutes, stirring all the time and removing the foam from the surface.

2. Spoon some jam on a plate and wait until thickened, if not continue boiling and testing until gelled. The jam should be thick enough to ladle it into the jars. 10 minutes before the jam is ready mix in the orange zest and orange juice.

3. Remove the saucepan from the heat and ladle freshly cooked jam into sterilized jars up to 1/5 inch from the top and seal the jars.

4. Flip the jars with the jam upside down or boil for around 10 minutes and then leave to cool. In case some of the jars with the blackcurrant jam are unsealed, place them into the fridge or reprocess the unsealed jars.

Nutritional Information (1 tbsp):

Calories: 53; Total fat: 4 oz; Total carbohydrates: 8 oz; Protein: 3 oz

# Orange-Redcurrant Jelly

***Prep Time: 50 min. | Makes: 6-7 11 oz jars***

Ingredients:

6 cups of redcurrants, fresh

3 tbsp. orange zest, minced

5 cups of sugar

3 tbsp. orange juice

How to Prepare:

1. Spoon 4 tbsp. sugar over the redcurrants and set aside for few hours and then crush the berries.

2. Pour some water and boil the redcurrants over low heat for 15-20 minutes, stirring all the time. Then strain the redcurrants to get 4 cups of the juice.

3. In a saucepan, combine the juice with the sugar and boil the juice for 30 minutes. The jelly should be thick enough to ladle it into the jars. Remove the foam from the surface. 10 minutes before the jelly is ready mix in the orange zest and orange juice.

4. Remove the saucepan from the heat and ladle the freshly cooked jelly into the sterilized jars and seal the jars.

5. Flip the jars upside down or boil for around 10 minutes and then leave to cool. Check the lids by pressing them with the finger. In case some of the jars with the redcurrant jelly are unsealed, place them into the fridge or reprocess the unsealed jars.

Nutritional Information (1 tbsp):

Calories: 56; Total fat: 3 oz; Total carbohydrates: 5 oz; Protein: 3 oz

# Pineapples & Apples Jam

***Prep Time: 40 min.*** | ***Makes: 4-5 10 oz jars***

Ingredients:

2 medium pineapples, peeled and diced

2 lbs big apples, peeled and sliced

4 cups of sugar

1 cup of water

1 tsp. Cinnamon

1 tsp. citric acid

How to Prepare:

1. Spoon the sugar over the fruits and set aside for few hours. Boil the pineapples and the apples with the sugar and the water over medium heat for around 40 minutes, stirring all the time until the sugar dissolves. Remove the foam from the surface.

2. The jam should be thick enough to spoon it into the jars. Few minutes before the jam is ready mix in the cinnamon and citric acid.

3. When the jam is ready, remove the saucepan from the heat and ladle freshly cooked jam into sterilized jars up to 1/5 inch from the top.

4. Seal the jars and then process them in a water bath. In a large pot, boil the jars for around 10 minutes and then take them out and leave to cool. Check the lids by pressing them with the finger. In case some of the jars are unsealed, place them into the fridge or reprocess the unsealed jars.

Nutritional Information (1 tbsp):

Calories: 53; Total fat: 7 oz; Total carbohydrates: 10 oz; Protein: 4 oz

# Lemon & Pears Jam

*Prep Time: 30 min. | Makes: 4-5 11 oz jars*

## Ingredients:

5 big pears, peeled and cubed

4 cups of sugar

half cup of lemon juice

1 tsp. vanilla

1 tsp. lemon zest, minced

## How to Prepare:

1. Boil the pears with the sugar, vanilla, lemon zest and lemon juice over medium heat for around 30 minutes, stirring all the time until the sugar dissolves. Remove the foam from the surface.

2. Spoon the freshly cooked jam into sterilized jars up to 1/5 inch from the top.

3. Seal the jars and then process them in a water bath. In a large pot, boil the jars for around 10 minutes and then take them out and leave to cool. Check the lids by pressing them with the finger. In case some of the jars with the lemon and pear jam are unsealed, place them into the fridge or reprocess the unsealed jars.

## Nutritional Information (1 tbsp):

Calories: 53; Total fat: 4 oz; Total carbohydrates: 10 oz; Protein: 2 oz

# Vanilla Gooseberry Jam

---

*Prep Time: 40 min.│ Makes around 6 11 oz jars*

---

Ingredients:

5 lb gooseberries

5 cups of sugar

3 tbsp. orange juice

2 tsp. vanilla

How to Prepare:

1. In a saucepan, combine the gooseberries with the sugar and leave for 2 hours unrefrigerated at room temperature.

2. Boil the berries with the sugar for 40 minutes, stirring until the sugar dissolves. Keep removing the foam and scum from the surface.

3. Five minutes before the jam is ready mix in the orange juice and vanilla and keep stirring until the gooseberries jam has thickened.

4. Ladle freshly cooked gooseberries jam into sterilized jars up to 1/4 inch from the top and then seal the jars.

5. Now flip the jars upside down and leave them for at least few hours or overnight to cool completely and only then turn them back. Check the lids by pressing them with the finger. In case some of the jars with the vanilla gooseberry jam are unsealed, place them into the fridge or reprocess the unsealed jars.

Nutritional Information (1 tbsp):

Calories: 59; Total fat: 1 oz; Total carbohydrates: 5.5 oz; Protein: 1 oz

# Vanilla Plum Jam

*Prep Time: 40 min. | Makes around 6 11 oz jars*

Ingredients:

5 lb plums, stoned

4 cups of sugar

1 tsp. citric acid

2 tsp. vanilla

How to Prepare:

1. Halve the plums and boil them with the sugar over medium heat for 40 minutes, stirring all the time and removing the foam from the surface.

2. Spoon some jam on a plate and wait until gelled, if not continue boiling and testing every few minutes. The vanilla plum jam should be thick and gelled enough to spoon it into the jars. Five minutes before the jam is ready mix in the citric acid and vanilla.

3. Remove the saucepan from the heat and spoon the freshly cooked jam into the sterilized jars up to 1/4 inch from the top and seal the jars.

4. Flip the jars with the vanilla plum jam upside down or boil them for around 10 minutes and then leave to cool. Check the lids by pressing them with the finger. In case some of the jars with the vanilla plum jam are unsealed, place them into the fridge or reprocess the unsealed jars.

Nutritional Information (1 tbsp):

Calories: 52; Total fat: 2 oz; Total carbohydrates: 7 oz; Protein: 1.5 oz

# Lemon-Almond Raspberry Jam

*Prep Time: 40 min.* | *Makes around 7 10 oz jars*

Ingredients:

8 cups of fresh raspberries, washed

1 tbsp. pure almonds extract

1 tbsp. pure vanilla extract

5 cups of sugar

1 tbsp. lemon juice

How to Prepare:

1. In a large pot, combine the raspberries with the sugar. Leave the raspberries for at least few hours unrefrigerated at room temperature or place into the fridge for 10 hours or overnight.

2. Boil the raspberries, and sugar over medium heat for around 40 minutes, stirring all the time until the sugar dissolves. Remove the foam from the raspberries jam. The best way to do that is to use a big spoon or ladle.

3. 10 minutes before the jam is ready pour the pure almonds extract, vanilla extract and lemon juice and keep stirring until the raspberries mixture has gelled. Pour one teaspoon of raspberry jam on a plate and wait until gelled, pressing with the finger or the spoon. If not continue boiling and testing every 5-10 minutes.

4. Remove the saucepan with the raspberries from the heat and pour freshly cooked jam into sterilized jars up to 1/5 inch from the top to seal the hot jars.

5. Flip the jars upside down or boil them for around 10 minutes and then leave to cool. Don't forget to check the lids by pressing them with the finger. In case some of the jars with the almond raspberry jam are unsealed, place them into the fridge or reprocess the unsealed jars.

Nutritional Information (1 tbsp):

Calories: 64; Total fat: 5 oz; Total carbohydrates: 10 oz; Protein: 2 oz

# Orange Jelly

*Prep Time: 1 hour│Makes: 8 10 oz jars*

Ingredients:

3 lb oranges

5 cups of sugar

2 tsp. vanilla

How to Prepare:

1. Squeeze the oranges. Spoon 1 cup of the sugar into the orange juice.

2. Boil the orange juice over the low heat for around 30 minutes, stirring all the time.

3. In a saucepan, combine the juice with the remaining sugar and boil the juice for 30 minutes until thickened. The jelly should be thick enough to pour it into the jars. Skim the foam from the surface. 10 minutes before the jelly is ready mix in the vanilla. Remove the saucepan from the heat and pour the freshly cooked jelly into the sterilized jars.

4. Turn the jars upside down or boil for around 10 minutes and then leave to cool. Check the lids by pressing them with the finger. In case some of the jars with the jelly are unsealed, place them into the fridge or reprocess the unsealed jars.

Nutritional Information (1 tbsp):
Calories: 57; Total fat: 4 oz; Total carbohydrates: 8 oz; Protein: 3 oz

# Lemon-Raspberry Jam

***Prep Time: 30 min. | Makes around 7 12 oz jars***

Ingredients:

3 lb raspberries

1 lemon, sliced

1 tsp. lemon zest, minced

6 cups of sugar

2 tbsp. lemon juice

How to Prepare:

1. In a saucepan, combine the raspberries and lemon slices and spoon the sugar over the fruits. Leave the raspberries for at least few hours unrefrigerated at room temperature.

2. Boil the raspberries and lemon slices over medium heat for around 30 minutes, stirring all the time with a spoon until the sugar dissolves but don't crush the berries or lemon slices. Remove the foam from the raspberry jam.

3. 10 min. before the jam is ready stir in the lemon zest and lemon juice and keep stirring until the raspberries and lemon mixture has gelled enough. Spoon some jam on a plate and wait until thickened, if not continue boiling and testing every 5 minutes.

4. Remove the saucepan with the raspberries from the heat and ladle freshly cooked jam into sterilized jars up to 1/5 inch from the top.

5. Flip the jars with the lemon raspberry jam upside down or boil for around 10 minutes and then leave to cool. Check the lids by pressing them with the finger. In case some of the jars with the lemon raspberry jam are unsealed, place them into the fridge or reprocess the unsealed jars.

Nutritional Information (1 tbsp):

Calories: 54; Total fat: 4 oz; Total carbohydrates: 8 oz; Protein: 3 oz

# Rose Petals & Cherry Jelly

---

*Prep Time: 1 hour | Makes: 6-7 11 oz jars*

---

Ingredients:

2 lbs cherries, pitted

2 cups of rose petals

5 cups of sugar

2 tsp. citric acid

How to Prepare:

1. Spoon 1 cup of the sugar over the berries and set aside for overnight. In a pan, heat the water and boil the rose petals on a low heat for about 15 minutes.

2. Boil the berries over the low heat for around 30 minutes, stirring all the time. Then mash the berries with the potato masher and strain the mixture to get 4-5 cups of the juice.

3. In a saucepan, combine the juice with the remaining sugar and rose petals. Boil the juice for 30 minutes until thickened. Pour the orange juice. The jelly should be thick enough to pour it into the jars. Skim the foam from the surface. 10 minutes before the jelly is ready mix in the citric acid.

4. Remove the saucepan from the heat and pour the freshly cooked jelly into the sterilized jars.

5. Turn the jars upside down or boil for around 10 minutes and then leave to cool. Check the lids by pressing them with the finger. In case some of the jars with the cherry jelly are unsealed, place them into the fridge or reprocess the unsealed jars.

Nutritional Information (1 tbsp):

Calories: 57; Total fat: 4 oz; Total carbohydrates: 8 oz; Protein: 3 oz

# Orange Jam

*Prep Time: 50 min.* | *Makes around 6 10 oz jars*

Ingredients:

2 lb oranges, peeled and diced

2 tbsp. gelatin or agar-agar substitute

5 cups of sugar

3 tsp. pure vanilla extract

How to Prepare:

1. In a big pot, combine the oranges, sugar, and pure vanilla extract and boil over medium heat for around 40 minutes, stirring all the time until the sugar dissolves. Remove the foam and the scum from the orange jam. Mix in the gelatin or vegetarian gelatin substitute and boil for 10 minutes.

2. Spoon some orange jam on a plate and wait until gelled. Check by pressing with the finger or the spoon, if not gelled enough continue boiling and testing every 5-10 minutes until gelled.

3. When the orange jam is ready, remove the pot from the heat and pour the freshly cooked jam into the sterilized and hot jars up to 1/4 inch from the top.

4. Seal the jars with the orange jam and flip them upside down or boil them for around 10 minutes and then leave to cool. Check the lids by pressing them with the finger. In case some of the jars with the orange jam are unsealed, place them into the fridge or reprocess the unsealed jars.

Nutritional Information (1 tbsp):
Calories: 58; Total fat: 4 oz; Total carbohydrates: 9 oz; Protein: 3 oz

# Lemon & Apples Jam

---

*Prep Time: 30 min.* | *Makes: 4-5 8 oz jars*

---

## Ingredients:

4 big apples, peeled and cubed

4 cups of sugar

half cup of lemon juice

1 tsp. vanilla

1 tsp. lemon zest, minced

## How to Prepare:

1. Boil the apples with the sugar, vanilla, lemon zest and lemon juice over medium heat for around 30 minutes, stirring all the time until the sugar dissolves. Remove the foam from the surface.

2. Spoon the freshly cooked jam into sterilized jars up to 1/5 inch from the top.

3. Seal the jars and then process them in a water bath. In a large pot, boil the jars for around 10 minutes and then take them out and leave to cool. Check the lids by pressing them with the finger. In case some of the jars with the jam are unsealed, place them into the fridge or reprocess the unsealed jars.

## Nutritional Information (1 tbsp):
Calories: 53; Total fat: 4 oz; Total carbohydrates: 10 oz; Protein: 2 oz

# Vanilla Apricot Jam

*Prep Time: 35 min.* | *Makes around 5 11 oz jars*

Ingredients:

6 cups of apricots, chopped

4 cups of sugar

2 tsp. lemon juice

2 tsp. vanilla

How to Prepare:

1. Wash and chop the apricots and place them into the pot and then mix in the sugar. Leave the apricots for at least few hours unrefrigerated at room temperature.

2. Boil the apricots over medium heat for around 30 minutes, stirring all the time until the sugar dissolves. Remember to remove the scum from the surface.

3. Mix in the lemon juice and vanilla and keep stirring until the apricots mixture has gelled. Put some apricot jam on the plate and press down with your finger to check the density. Continue boiling and testing every five or ten minutes until thickened enough to spoon it into the jars.

4. Remove the pot with the apricot jam from the heat and carefully spoon freshly cooked jam into the hot and sterilized jars up to 1/5 inch from the top.

5. Seal the jars and then turn them upside down or boil for around 10 minutes and then leave to cool. Check the lids by pressing them with the finger. In case some of the jars with the apricot jam are unsealed, place them into the fridge or reprocess the unsealed jars.

Nutritional Information (1 tbsp):

Calories: 60; Total fat: 2 oz; Total carbohydrates: 5 oz; Protein: 0.8 oz

# Pumpkin & Orange Jam

***Prep Time: 45 min. | Makes around 6 10 oz jars***

Ingredients:

2 lb pumpkin, peeled and cubed

3 cups of sugar

1 cup of brown

2 cups of orange juice

2 tsp. citric acid

1 tsp. vanilla

How to Prepare:

1. Spoon the white sugar over the cubed pumpkin and leave for at least few hours unrefrigerated at room temperature or place in the fridge overnight.

2. In a pot, boil the pumpkin for around 45 minutes on medium heat, stirring until the sugar dissolves. Stir in the brown sugar and orange juice. Pumpkin should be soft. Remember to remove the foam from the surface. Five minutes before the pumpkin jam is ready mix in the citric acid and vanilla. The pumpkin jam should be gelled enough to ladle it into the jars.

3. Ladle the freshly boiled pumpkin jam into the sterilized and hot jars and seal the jars.

4. Flip the jars upside down or boil for around 10 minutes and then leave to cool. In case some of the jars with the pumpkin jam are unsealed, place them into the fridge or reprocess the unsealed jars.

Nutritional Information (1 tbsp):

Calories: 51; Total fat: 2 oz; Total carbohydrates: 4 oz; Protein: 1 oz

# Apple-Peach Jam

---

*Prep Time: 50 min.* | *Makes: 7-8 12 oz jars*

---

## Ingredients:

2-2.5 lb apples, diced

2 lb peaches, diced

1 tbsp. orange zest, minced

4 cups of sugar

1 tsp. citric acid

## How to Prepare:

1. Spoon the sugar over the apples and peaches and set aside for at least few hours.

2. Boil the apples and peaches with the sugar on a medium heat for around 40 minutes, stirring all the time until thickened. Remove the scum from the surface. Few minutes before the jam is ready mix in the orange zest and citric acid.

3. Spoon the apple jam into the sterilized jars up to 1/4 inch from the top and seal the jars. Then flip the jars upside down or boil for around 10 minutes and then leave to cool. Check the lids by pressing them with the finger. In case some of the jars with the apple-peach jam are unsealed, place them into the fridge or reprocess the unsealed jars.

## Nutritional Information (1 tbsp):

Calories: 56; Total fat: 5 oz; Total carbohydrates: 8 oz; Protein: 4 oz

# Mango-Pears Jam

*Prep Time: 50 min.* | *Makes: 3-4 10 oz jars*

Ingredients:

2 lb pears, peeled and diced

3 medium mangos, peeled and diced

4 cups of sugar

5 tbsp. orange juice

How to Prepare:

1. Spoon the sugar over the pears and set aside for at least few hours.

2. Boil the pears and mangos with the sugar on a medium heat for 40 minutes, stirring all the time until thickened. Remove the scum from the surface. Few minutes before the jam is ready mix in the orange juice.

3. Ladle the pears jam into the sterilized jars up to 1/4 inch from the top and seal the jars. Then flip the jars upside down or boil for around 10 minutes and then leave to cool. Check the lids by pressing them with the finger. In case some of the jars with the jam are unsealed, place them into the fridge or reprocess the unsealed jars.

Nutritional Information (1 tbsp):

Calories: 56; Total fat: 6 oz; Total carbohydrates: 10 oz; Protein: 5 oz

# Apple Jelly with Raspberries

*Prep Time: 50 min.* | *Makes: 7 10 oz jars*

## Ingredients:

5 cups of sweet apple juice

1 cup of raspberry syrup

2 tbsp. gelatin or agar-agar substitute

2 cups of sugar

## How to Prepare:

1. Boil the apple juice with the raspberry syrup over the low heat for around 20 minutes, stirring all the time. Spoon the sugar and gelatin. Boil the juice for 30 minutes until thickened. The jelly should be thick enough to pour it into the jars. Skim the foam from the surface.

2. Remove the saucepan from the heat and pour the freshly cooked jelly into the sterilized jars.

3. Turn the jars upside down or boil for around 10 minutes and then leave to cool. Check the lids by pressing them with the finger. In case some of the jars with the jelly are unsealed, place them into the fridge or reprocess the unsealed jars.

## Nutritional Information (1 tbsp):

Calories: 57; Total fat: 7 oz; Total carbohydrates: 10 oz; Protein: 5 oz

# Pineapple Jelly with Raspberries

*Prep Time: 50 min. | Makes: 5-6 8 oz jars*

Ingredients:

25 oz pineapple juice

1 cup of raspberry syrup

2 tbsp. gelatin or agar-agar substitute

2 cups of sugar

How to Prepare:

1. Boil the pineapple juice with the raspberry syrup over the low heat for around 20 minutes, stirring all the time. Spoon the sugar and gelatin. Boil the juice for 30 minutes until thickened. The jelly should be thick enough to pour it into the jars. Skim the foam from the surface.

2. Remove the saucepan from the heat and pour the freshly cooked jelly into the sterilized jars.

3. Turn the jars upside down or boil for around 10 minutes and then leave to cool. Check the lids by pressing them with the finger. In case some of the jars with the jelly are unsealed, place them into the fridge or reprocess the unsealed jars.

Nutritional Information (1 tbsp):

Calories: 55; Total fat: 8 oz; Total carbohydrates: 9 oz; Protein: 4 oz

# Cherry Jam with Blueberries

---

*Prep Time: 40 min.* | *Makes around 6 10 oz jars*

---

Ingredients:

2 lbs cherries, pitted

5 cups of blueberries, fresh

5 cups of sugar

3 tsp. vanilla

How to Prepare:

1. In a big pot, combine the cherries, blueberries, sugar, and vanilla and boil over the medium heat for around 40 minutes, stirring all the time until the sugar dissolves. Remove the foam and the scum from the cherry jam.

2. Spoon some cherry jam on a plate and wait until gelled. Check by pressing with the finger or the spoon, if not gelled enough continue boiling and testing every 5-10 minutes until gelled.

3. When the cherry jam is ready, remove the pot with the cherries from the heat and pour the freshly cooked jam into the sterilized and hot jars up to 1/4 inch from the top.

4. Seal the jars with the jam and flip them upside down or boil them for around 10 minutes and then leave to cool. Check the lids by pressing them with the finger. In case some of the jars with the jam are unsealed, place them into the fridge or reprocess the unsealed jars.

Nutritional Information (1 tbsp):

Calories: 62; Total fat: 4 oz; Total carbohydrates: 12 oz; Protein: 3 oz

# Fig Jam with Bananas

---

*Prep Time: 40 min. | Makes around 10 10 oz jars*

---

Ingredients:

2 lb figs, diced

5 bananas, diced

1 cups of brown sugar

2 tsp. pure vanilla extract

2 tsp. citric acid

How to Prepare:

1. Place the diced figs into a big saucepan and spoon the sugar on top. Leave for at least few hours unrefrigerated at room temperature or place in the fridge overnight.

2. Then boil the figs over the medium heat for around 10 minutes, stirring all the time until the sugar dissolves. Remove the foam from the surface. Then reduce the heat and continue to boil for around 30 minutes.

3. Mix in the pure vanilla extract, citric acid, and bananas and keep stirring until the figs mixture has gelled and thickened. Pour some jam on a plate and check if gelled, pressing it with the finger, if not continue boiling and testing.

4. Remove the saucepan with the fig jam from the heat and pour the freshly cooked jam into the sterilized and hot jars up to 1/5 inch from the top.

5. Seal the jars and then turn them upside down. Leave the jars for overnight to cool completely and only then turn them back.

6. Or you can do it by processing the jars in the water bath and boiling them for around 10 minutes and then leaving to cool. It is important to remember to check the lids by pressing them with the finger. In case some of the jars with the fig jam are unsealed, place them into the fridge or reprocess the unsealed jars.

Nutritional Information (1 tbsp):

Calories: 78; Total fat: 10 oz; Total carbohydrates: 12 oz; Protein: 7 oz

# Rose Petal & Raspberry Jelly

***Prep Time: 50 min.*** | ***Makes: 6-7 11 oz jars***

Ingredients:

30 oz raspberries, fresh

5 oz fresh rose petals

5 cups of sugar

3 tbsp. pure vanilla extract

1 tbsp. citric acid or lemon juice

How to Prepare:

1. Spoon 4 tbsp. sugar over the raspberries and set aside for few hours. Then mash the berries using the potato masher.

2. In a pan, heat the water and boil the rose petals on a low heat for about 15 minutes.

3. Pour some water and boil the raspberries over the low heat for around 15-20 minutes, stirring all the time. Then strain the raspberries to get 4 cups of the juice.

4. In a saucepan, combine the juice with the sugar and rose petals. Boil the juice for 30 minutes. The jelly should be thick enough to pour it into the jars. Add the vanilla and citric acid.

5. Remove the saucepan from the heat and ladle the freshly cooked jelly into the sterilized jars and seal the jars.

6. Flip the jars upside down or boil for around 10 minutes and then leave to cool. Check the lids by pressing them with the finger. In case some of the jars with the rose petal jelly are unsealed, place them into the fridge or reprocess the unsealed jars.

Nutritional Information (1 tbsp):

Calories: 55; Total fat: 4 oz; Total carbohydrates: 10 oz; Protein: 4 oz

# Pineapple Taste Redcurrant Jam

*Prep Time: 40 min.* | *Makes around 5-6 10 oz jars*

Ingredients:

30 oz redcurrants

5 cups of sugar

2 tbsp. lime juice

3 tsp. pure pineapple extract

How to Prepare:

1. In a large pot, boil the redcurrants over medium heat for about 40 minutes, stirring until the sugar dissolves. Skim the foam from the jam.

2. Ten minutes before the redcurrants jam is ready, mix in the lime juice and pure pineapple extract and keep stirring until the redcurrants mixture has gelled enough. Continue boiling and testing every five minutes until the jam gets thick enough to ladle it into the jars.

3. Remove the saucepan with the redcurrants from the heat and ladle freshly cooked jam into the hot and sterilized jars up to 1/5 inch from the top.

4.  Flip the jars with the redcurrants jam upside down or boil for around 10 minutes and then leave to cool. Check the lids by pressing them with the finger. In case some of the jars with the redcurrants jam are unsealed, place them into the fridge or reprocess the unsealed jars.

**Nutritional Information (1 tbsp):**
Calories: 48; Total fat: 4 oz; Total carbohydrates: 5 oz; Protein: 2 oz

# Oranges Jelly

*Prep Time: 1 hour│ Makes: 8 10 oz jars*

**Ingredients:**

3 lb oranges, peeled and diced

5 cups of sugar

2 tsp. vanilla

**How to Prepare:**

1. Spoon 1 cup of the sugar over the oranges. Set aside for overnight.

2. Boil the oranges over the low heat for around 30 minutes, stirring all the time. Pour in some water. Then mash the oranges using the potato masher and strain the mixture to get 4-5 cups of the juice.

3. In a saucepan, combine the juice with the remaining sugar and boil the juice for 30 minutes until thickened. The jelly should be thick enough to pour it into the jars. Skim the foam from the surface. 10 minutes before the jelly is ready mix in the vanilla.

4. Remove the saucepan from the heat and pour the freshly cooked jelly into the sterilized jars.

5. Turn the jars upside down or boil for around 10 minutes and then leave to cool. Check the lids by pressing them with the finger. In case some of the jars with the jelly are unsealed, place them into the fridge or reprocess the unsealed jars.

**Nutritional Information (1 tbsp):**

Calories: 57; Total fat: 4 oz; Total carbohydrates: 8 oz; Protein: 3 oz

# Blueberry Orange Jelly

*Prep Time: 1 hour│Makes: 8 10 oz jars*

**Ingredients:**

3 lbs blueberries

4 oranges, peeled and diced

5 cups of sugar

2 tsp. citric acid

**How to Prepare:**

1. Spoon 1 cup of the sugar over the berries and oranges. Set aside for overnight.

2. Boil the blueberries and oranges over the low heat for around 30 minutes, stirring all the time. Pour in some water. Then mash the blueberries with the potato masher and strain the mixture to get 4-5 cups of the juice.

3. In a saucepan, combine the juice with the remaining sugar and boil the juice for 30 minutes until thickened. The jelly should be thick enough to pour it into the jars. Skim the foam from the surface. 10 minutes before the jelly is ready mix in the citric acid.

4. Remove the saucepan from the heat and pour the freshly cooked jelly into the sterilized jars.

5. Turn the jars upside down or boil for around 10 minutes and then leave to cool. Check the lids by pressing them with the finger. In case some of the jars with the jelly are unsealed, place them into the fridge or reprocess the unsealed jars.

**Nutritional Information (1 tbsp):**

Calories: 57; Total fat: 4 oz; Total carbohydrates: 8 oz; Protein: 3 oz

# Gooseberry-Orange Jam

*Prep Time: 50 min.* | *Makes: 7-8 10 oz jars*

Ingredients:

2 lb gooseberries

2 medium oranges, diced

4 cups of brown sugar

3 tbsp. orange juice, squeezed

2 tsp. vanilla

How to Prepare:

1. Spoon the gooseberries into a big saucepan and mix in the sugar and vanilla. Leave for at least 6 hours unrefrigerated at room temperature or place in the fridge overnight.

2. In the same saucepan boil the gooseberries and sugar-vanilla mixture over the high heat for around 10 minutes, stirring all the time with a spoon until the sugar dissolves.

3. Then add in the oranges. Reduce the heat and continue to boil for around 40 minutes but don't forget to skim the foam from the berries.

4. Pour the orange juice. Keep stirring until the berries mixture has gelled and thickened.

5. Remove the saucepan with the gooseberries from the heat and pour the freshly cooked jam into the sterilized jars up to 1/5 inch from the top.

6. Seal the jars and then turn the jars upside down. Leave them for overnight to cool completely and only then turn them back.

Nutritional Information (1 tbsp):

Calories: 68; Total fat: 3 oz; Total carbohydrates: 8 oz; Protein: 2 oz

# Orange Cherry Jelly

---

*Prep Time: 1 hour | Makes: 6-7 11 oz jars*

---

Ingredients:

2 lbs cherries, pitted

2 cups of orange juice

5 cups of sugar

2 tsp. citric acid

How to Prepare:

1. Spoon 1 cup of sugar over the berries and set aside for overnight.

2. Boil the berries over the low heat for around 30 minutes, stirring all the time. Then mash the berries with the potato masher and strain the mixture to get 4-5 cups of the juice.

3. In a saucepan, combine the juice with the remaining sugar and boil the juice for 30 minutes until thickened. Pour the orange juice. The jelly should be thick enough to pour it into the jars. Skim the foam from the surface. 10 minutes before the jelly is ready mix in the citric acid.

4. Remove the saucepan from the heat and pour the freshly cooked jelly into the sterilized jars.

5. Turn the jars upside down or boil for around 10 minutes and then leave to cool. Check the lids by pressing them with the finger. In case some of the jars with the cherry jelly are unsealed, place them into the fridge or reprocess the unsealed jars.

Nutritional Information (1 tbsp):

Calories: 57; Total fat: 4 oz; Total carbohydrates: 8 oz; Protein: 3 oz

# Cherry Jelly with Raspberries and Oranges

---

*Prep Time: 1 hour⏐ Makes: 8 10 oz jars*

---

**Ingredients:**

2 lbs cherries, pitted

2 lbs raspberries

4 oranges, peeled and diced

5 cups of sugar

2 tsp. citric acid

**How to Prepare:**

1. Spoon 1 cup of the sugar over the berries and oranges. Set aside for overnight.

2. Boil the berries and oranges over the low heat for around 30 minutes, stirring all the time. Pour in some water. Then mash the berries using the potato masher and strain the mixture to get 4-5 cups of the juice.

3. In a saucepan, combine the juice with the remaining sugar and boil the juice for 30 minutes until thickened. The jelly should be thick enough to pour it into the jars. Skim the foam from the surface. 10 minutes before the jelly is ready mix in the citric acid.

4. Remove the saucepan from the heat and pour the freshly cooked jelly into the sterilized jars.

5. Turn the jars upside down or boil for around 10 minutes and then leave to cool. Check the lids by pressing them with the finger. In case some of the jars with the jelly are unsealed, place them into the fridge or reprocess the unsealed jars.

**Nutritional Information (1 tbsp):**

Calories: 57; Total fat: 4 oz; Total carbohydrates: 8 oz; Protein: 3 oz

# Banana Taste Redcurrant Jam

---

*Prep Time: 40 min.* | *Makes around 5-6 10 oz jars*

---

Ingredients:

30 oz redcurrants

5 cups of sugar

2 tbsp. lime juice

3 tsp. pure banana extract

How to Prepare:

1. In a large pot, boil the redcurrants over medium heat for about 40 minutes, stirring until the sugar dissolves. Skim the foam from the jam.

2. Ten minutes before the redcurrants jam is ready, mix in the lime juice and pure banana extract and keep stirring until the redcurrants mixture has gelled enough. Continue boiling and testing every five minutes until the jam gets thick enough to ladle it into the jars.

3. Remove the saucepan with the redcurrants from the heat and ladle freshly cooked jam into the hot and sterilized jars up to 1/5 inch from the top.

4. Flip the jars with the redcurrants jam upside down or boil for around 10 minutes and then leave to cool. Check the lids by pressing them with the finger. In case some of the jars with the redcurrants jam are unsealed, place them into the fridge or reprocess the unsealed jars.

Nutritional Information (1 tbsp):
Calories: 48; Total fat: 4 oz; Total carbohydrates: 5 oz; Protein: 2 oz

# Cashews Gooseberry Jam

***Prep Time: 50 min.*** | ***Makes: 7-8 10 oz jars***

## Ingredients:

2 lb gooseberries

1 cup of cashews

4 cups of brown sugar

3 tbsp. lemon juice, squeezed

2 tsp. vanilla

## How to Prepare:

1. Grind the cashews. In a bowl, combine the sugar with the vanilla and mix well.

2. Then place the gooseberries into a big saucepan and spoon the sugar-vanilla mixture on top and leave for at least 6 hours unrefrigerated at room temperature or place in the fridge overnight.

3. In the same saucepan boil the gooseberries and sugar-vanilla mixture over high heat for around 10 minutes, stirring all the time with a spoon until sugar dissolves.

4. Then reduce the heat and continue to boil for around 40 minutes but don't forget to skim the foam from the berries.

5. Pour the lemon juice and add the nuts. Keep stirring until the berries mixture has gelled and thickened.

6. Remove the saucepan with the gooseberries from the heat and pour the freshly cooked jam into the sterilized jars up to 1/5 inch from the top.

7. Seal the jars and then turn the jars upside down. Leave them for overnight to cool completely and only then turn them back.

## Nutritional Information (1 tbsp):

Calories: 67; Total fat: 1 oz; Total carbohydrates: 4 oz; Protein: 0.8 oz

# Melon & Orange Jelly

*Prep Time: 1 hour* | *Makes: 8 10 oz jars*

## Ingredients:

2 lb oranges, peeled and diced

1 medium melon (20 0z), peeled and diced

5 cups of sugar

2 tsp. pure vanilla extract

## How to Prepare:

1. Spoon 1 cup of the sugar over the oranges. Set aside for overnight.

2. Boil the oranges over the low heat for around 30 minutes, stirring all the time. Pour in some water. Then mash the oranges the potato masher and strain the mixture to get 4-5 cups of the juice.

3. In a saucepan, combine the juice with the remaining sugar and melon. Boil the juice for 30 minutes until thickened. The jelly should be thick enough to pour it into the jars. Skim the foam from the surface. 10 minutes before the jelly is ready mix in the vanilla.

4. Remove the saucepan from the heat and pour the freshly cooked jelly into the sterilized jars.

5. Turn the jars upside down or boil for around 10 minutes and then leave to cool. Check the lids by pressing them with the finger. In case some of the jars with the jelly are unsealed, place them into the fridge or reprocess the unsealed jars.

## Nutritional Information (1 tbsp):

Calories: 54; Total fat: 4 oz; Total carbohydrates: 7 oz; Protein: 3 oz

# Pineapple Jam

*Prep Time: 40 min.* | *Makes around 10 10 oz jars*

Ingredients:

2 lb pineapples, peeled and diced

1 cups of brown sugar

2 tsp. pure pineapple extract

2 tsp. citric acid

2 tsp. vanilla

How to Prepare:

1. Place the diced pineapples into a big saucepan and spoon the sugar on top. Leave for at least few hours unrefrigerated at room temperature or place in the fridge overnight.

2. Then boil the pineapples over the medium heat for around 10 minutes, stirring all the time until the sugar dissolves. Remove the foam from the surface. Then reduce the heat and continue to boil for around 30 minutes.

3. Mix in the pure pineapple extract, citric acid, and vanilla and keep stirring until the pineapples mixture has gelled and thickened. Pour some jam on a plate and check if gelled, pressing it with the finger, if not continue boiling and testing.

4. Remove the saucepan with the pineapples from the heat and pour the freshly cooked jam into the sterilized and hot jars up to 1/5 inch from the top.

5. Seal the jars and then turn the jars upside down. Leave them for overnight to cool completely and only then turn them back.

6. Or you can do it by processing the jars in the water bath and boiling them for around 10 minutes and then leaving to cool. It is important to remember to check the lids by pressing them with the finger. In case some of the jars with the pineapple jam are unsealed, place them into the fridge or reprocess the unsealed jars.

Nutritional Information (1 tbsp):

Calories: 72; Total fat: 6 oz; Total carbohydrates: 10 oz; Protein: 5 oz

# Rose Petal & Blackcurrant Jelly

---

*Prep Time: 50 min. | Makes: 6-7 11 oz jars*

---

## Ingredients:

25 oz blackcurrants, fresh

5 oz fresh rose petals

5 cups of sugar

3 tbsp. pure vanilla extract

## How to Prepare:

1. Spoon 4 tbsp. sugar over the blackcurrants and set aside for few hours and then mash the berries using the potato masher.

2. In a pan, heat the water and boil the rose petals on a low heat for about 15 minutes.

3. Pour some water and boil the redcurrants over the low heat for around 15-20 minutes, stirring all the time. Then strain the blackcurrants to get 4 cups of the juice.

4. In a saucepan, combine the juice with the sugar and rose petals. Boil the juice for 30 minutes. The jelly should be thick enough to pour it into the jars.

5. Remove the saucepan from the heat and ladle the freshly cooked jelly into the sterilized jars and seal the jars.

6. Flip the jars upside down or boil for around 10 minutes and then leave to cool. Check the lids by pressing them with the finger. In case some of the jars with the rose petal and blackcurrant jelly are unsealed, place them into the fridge or reprocess the unsealed jars.

## Nutritional Information (1 tbsp):

Calories: 54; Total fat: 2 oz; Total carbohydrates: 9 oz; Protein: 3 oz

# Plum Jelly with Kiwi

---

*Prep Time: 1 hour | Makes: 6-7 11 oz jars*

---

## Ingredients:

4 lbs plums, pitted

5 kiwis, peeled and sliced

5 cups of sugar

2 tsp. citric acid

## How to Prepare:

1. Spoon 1 cup of sugar over the plums and set aside for overnight.

2. Pour some water and boil the plums over the low heat for around 30 minutes, stirring all the time. Then mash the plums with the potato masher and strain the mixture to get 4-5 cups of the juice.

3. In a saucepan, combine the juice with the remaining sugar and kiwi. Boil the juice for 30 minutes until thickened. The jelly should be thick enough to pour it into the jars. Skim the foam from the surface. 10 minutes before the jelly is ready mix in the citric acid.

4. Remove the saucepan from the heat and pour the freshly cooked jelly into the sterilized jars.

5. Turn the jars upside down or boil for around 10 minutes and then leave to cool. Check the lids by pressing them with the finger. In case some of the jars with the plum jelly are unsealed, place them into the fridge or reprocess the unsealed jars.

## Nutritional Information (1 tbsp):

Calories: 65; Total fat: 5 oz; Total carbohydrates: 7 oz; Protein: 3 oz

# Lemon Taste Blackberry Jelly

---

*Prep Time: 50 min.* | *Makes: 7-8 10 oz jars*

---

Ingredients:

25 oz blackberries, fresh

5 cups of sugar

2 medium lemons, halved and squeezed

3 tbsp. pure vanilla extract

How to Prepare:

1. Spoon 4 tbsp. sugar over the blackberries. Set aside for few hours. Then mash the blackberries using the potato masher.

2. Pour some water and boil the blackberries on a low heat for around 15-20 minutes, stirring all the time. Then strain the blackberries to get 4 cups of the juice.

3. In a saucepan, combine the juice with the sugar and pure vanilla extract. Pour the lemon juice. Boil the blackberry juice for 30 minutes. The jelly should be thick enough to pour it into the jars.

4. Remove the saucepan from the heat and ladle the freshly cooked jelly into the sterilized jars and seal the jars.

5. Flip the jars upside down or boil for around 10 minutes and then leave to cool. Check the lids by pressing them with the finger. In case some of the jars with the blackberry jelly are unsealed, place them into the fridge or reprocess the unsealed jars.

Nutritional Information (1 tbsp):

Calories: 52; Total fat: 4 oz; Total carbohydrates: 9 oz; Protein: 3 oz

# Alpine Strawberry Tangerine Jam

---

***Prep Time: 40 min.*** | ***Makes: 3-4 10 oz jars***

---

## Ingredients:

2-2.5 lb Alpine strawberries

1 lb tangerines

4 cups of sugar

1 tbsp. orange juice

## How to Prepare:

1.  Spoon the sugar over the Alpine strawberries and set aside for at least few hours.

2.  Boil the Alpine strawberries with the sugar and tangerines over medium heat for 40 minutes, stirring all the time until thickened. Remove the scum from the surface. Few minutes before the jam is ready mix in the orange zest and orange juice.

3.  Pour the Alpine strawberry jam into sterilized jars up to 1/4 inch from the top and seal the jars. Then flip the jars upside down or boil for around 10 minutes and then leave to cool. Check the lids by pressing them with the finger. In case some of the jars with the Alpine strawberry orange jam are unsealed, place them into the fridge or reprocess the unsealed jars.

## Nutritional Information (1 tbsp):

Calories: 53; Total fat: 2 oz; Total carbohydrates: 7 oz; Protein: 3 oz

# Tangerine & Pineapple Jelly

*Prep Time: 50 min.* | *Makes: 8 10 oz jars*

Ingredients:

1 lb tangerines

1 lb pineapple, peeled and diced

1 tbsp. gelatin

5 cups of sugar

1 cup of pineapple juice

How to Prepare:

1. Spoon the 1 cup of the sugar over the fruits. Set aside for overnight.

2. Boil the fruits over the low heat for around 20 minutes, stirring all the time. Pour in some water. Then mash the fruits using the potato masher and strain the mixture to get 4-5 cups of the juice.

3. In a saucepan, combine the juice with the remaining sugar, pineapple juice and gelatin and boil for 30 minutes until thickened. The jelly should be thick enough to pour it into the jars. Skim the foam from the surface. 10 minutes before the jelly is ready mix in the citric acid.

4. Remove the saucepan from the heat and pour the freshly cooked jelly into the sterilized jars.

5. Turn the jars upside down or boil for around 10 minutes and then leave to cool. Check the lids by pressing them with the finger. In case some of the jars with the jelly are unsealed, place them into the fridge or reprocess the unsealed jars.

Nutritional Information (1 tbsp):

Calories: 52; Total fat: 6 oz; Total carbohydrates: 9 oz; Protein: 4 oz

# Peach Jam with Mango and Kiwi

*__Prep Time: 40 min.__ | __Makes: 5-6 11 oz jars__*

### Ingredients:

3 lb peaches, pitted and diced

1 lb mango, peeled and diced

25 oz kiwi's, peeled and diced

5 cups of sugar

1 tbsp. citric acid

### How to Prepare:

1. Spoon the sugar over the peaches, mangos and kiwis and set aside for few hours. Boil the fruits over medium heat for around 40 minutes, stirring all the time. Remove the foam from the surface and stir in the citric acid.

2. Pour 1 tbs. of fruit jam on a plate and wait until thickened, if not continue boiling and testing. The jam should be thick enough to ladle it into the jars.

3. Remove the saucepan from the heat and ladle the freshly cooked jam into the sterilized jars up to 1/5 inch from the top and seal the jars.

4. Then flip the jars upside down or boil for around 10 minutes and then leave to cool. Check the lids by pressing them with the finger. In case some of the jars with the cherry jam are unsealed, place them into the fridge or reprocess the unsealed jars.

### Nutritional Information (1 tbsp):

Calories: 50; Total fat: 2 oz; Total carbohydrates: 6 oz; Protein: 1 oz

# Redcurrant Jelly with Pears

---

### *Prep Time: 50 min. | Makes: 6-7 11 oz jars*

---

Ingredients:

2 lb redcurrants, fresh

1 lb pears, halved

1 tbsp. gelatin

5 cups of sugar


How to Prepare:

1.  Spoon 4 tbsp. sugar over the redcurrants and set aside for few hours and then crush the berries.

2.  Pour some water and boil the redcurrants over the low heat for 15-20 minutes, stirring all the time. Then strain the redcurrants to get 4 cups of the juice.

3.  In a saucepan, combine the juice with the halved pears and sugar. Boil the juice for 30 minutes. 10 minutes before the jelly is ready mix in the gelatin. The jelly should be thick enough to ladle it into the jars.

4.  Remove the saucepan from the heat and ladle the freshly cooked jelly into the sterilized jars and seal the jars.

5.  Flip the jars upside down or boil for around 10 minutes and then leave to cool. Check the lids by pressing them with the finger. In case some of the jars with the redcurrant jelly are unsealed, place them into the fridge or reprocess the unsealed jars.

Nutritional Information (1 tbsp):

Calories: 57; Total fat: 4 oz; Total carbohydrates: 11 oz; Protein: 3 oz

# Blackcurrant Jam with Apricots

---

*Prep Time: 40 min.* | *Makes: 5-6 11 oz jars*

---

## Ingredients:

4 cups of blackcurrants, fresh

1 lb apricots, pitted and diced

6 cups of sugar

1 tsp. vanilla

## How to Prepare:

1. Wash the blackcurrants and boil the berries with the apricots and sugar over the medium heat for 40 minutes, stirring all the time until thickened. Remove the foam from the surface.

2. Spoon some jam on a plate and wait until thickened, if not continue boiling and testing. The jam should be thick enough to spoon it into the jars. Few minutes before the jam is ready stir in the vanilla.

3. When the jam is ready, remove the saucepan from the heat and ladle the freshly cooked blackcurrant jam into sterilized jars up to 1/5 inch from the top and seal the jars.

4. Flip the jars with the blackcurrant jam upside down or boil for around 10 minutes and then leave to cool. Check the lids by pressing them with the finger. In case some of the jars with the blackcurrant jam are unsealed, place them into the fridge or reprocess the unsealed jars.

## Nutritional Information (1 tbsp):

Calories: 66; Total fat: 6 oz; Total carbohydrates: 12 oz; Protein: 3 oz

# Plum and Blackcurrant Jelly

*Prep Time: 55 min. | Makes: 7-8 12 oz jars*

## Ingredients:

7 cups of blackcurrants, fresh

1 lbs plums, pitted

4 cups of sugar

1 tsp. citric acid

1 tsp. vanilla

## How to Prepare:

1. Spoon 4 tbsp. sugar over the blackcurrants and plums. Set aside for few hours and then mash the berries using the potatoes masher.

2. Pour some water and boil the blackcurrants and plums over low heat for 20-25 minutes, stirring all the time. Then strain the blackcurrants and plums to get 4-5 cups of the juice.

3. In a saucepan, combine the juice with the sugar and vanilla and boil the juice for 30 minutes. The jelly should be thick enough to ladle it into the jars. Remove the foam from the surface.

4. Remove the saucepan from the heat and ladle the freshly cooked jelly into the sterilized jars and seal the jars.

5. Flip the jars upside down or boil for around 10 minutes and then leave to cool. In case some of the jars with the blackcurrant jelly are unsealed, place them into the fridge or reprocess the unsealed jars.

## Nutritional Information (1 tbsp):

Calories: 55; Total fat: 6 oz; Total carbohydrates: 13 oz; Protein: 4 oz

# Baked Vanilla Cherry Jam

---

*Prep Time: 2 hours │ Makes around 7 11 oz jars*

---

Ingredients:

6 lb cherry, stoned

1 cup of water

5 cups of sugar

3 tsp. vanilla

baking spray or unsalted butter

How to Prepare:

1. Combine the stoned cherries with the sugar and preheat the oven to 300°-360° Fahrenheit and then coat the baking pan with the baking spray or unsalted butter.

2. Pour one cup of water and mix in three teaspoons vanilla and bake the cherries for around 1.5-2 hours until thickened and gelled enough to spoon the cherry jam into the jars. If the jam is not gelled enough continue baking and testing every five or ten minutes. The jam should be gelled enough to spoon it into the jars.

3. Spoon the freshly baked cherry jam into the sterilized and hot jars up to 1/5 inch from the top and seal the jars.

4. Flip the jars upside down or boil for around 10 minutes and then leave to cool. Check the lids by pressing them with the finger. In case some of the jars with the cherry jam are unsealed, place them into the fridge or reprocess the unsealed jars.

Nutritional Information (1 tbsp):

Calories: 58; Total fat: 7 oz; Total carbohydrates: 13 oz; Protein: 3 oz

# Baked Apple-Pear Jam

*Prep Time: 50 min.│Makes around 7 11 oz jars*

Ingredients:

5 lb sweet pears, peeled and cubed

5 lb apples, cubed

4 cups of sugar

5 tbsp. lemon juice

1 tbsp. cinnamon

baking spray or butter

How to Prepare:

1. Spoon the sugar and pour the lemon juice over the pears and apples. Set aside for around 2 to 3 hours unrefrigerated at room temperature.

2. Preheat the oven to 300°-350° Fahrenheit and then coat the baking pan with the baking spray or butter.

3. Spoon the cinnamon over the pears and apples. Then bake the pears and apples with the sugar, lemon juice, and cinnamon for around 40 minutes until thickened and gelled enough, if not continue baking and testing every five to ten minutes. The apple-pear jam should be gelled enough to ladle it into the jars.

4. When the apple-pear jam is ready ladle the freshly baked jam into the sterilized and hot jars up to 1/4 inch from the top and then seal the jars.

5. Flip the jars upside down or boil for around 10 minutes and then leave to cool. Check the lids by pressing them with the finger. In case some of the jars with the apple-pear jam are unsealed, place them into the fridge or reprocess the unsealed jars.

Nutritional Information (1 tbsp):

Calories: 45; Total fat: 5 oz; Total carbohydrates: 13 oz; Protein: 3 oz

# Baked Pear Orange Jam

*Prep Time: 50 min.│Makes around 8 11 oz jars*

Ingredients:

6 lb sweet pears, peeled and cubed

1 lb oranges, cubed

5 cups of sugar

3 tbsp. orange zest, minced

1 cup of orange juice

1 tbsp. cinnamon

baking spray or butter

How to Prepare:

1.  Wash and peel the pears and then cube them. Spoon the sugar and pour one cup of the orange juice over the pears and set aside for around 2 to 3 hours unrefrigerated at room temperature. Preheat the oven to 300°-350° Fahrenheit and then coat the baking pan with the baking spray or butter.

2.  Spoon the cinnamon and orange zest over the pears. Then bake the pears with the oranges, sugar, orange juice, and cinnamon for around 50 minutes until thickened and gelled enough, if not continue baking and testing every five to ten minutes. The pear orange jam should be gelled enough to ladle it into the jars. When the pear orange jam is ready ladle the freshly baked jam into the sterilized and hot jars up to 1/5 inch from the top and then seal the jars.

3.  Flip the jars upside down or boil for around 10 minutes and then leave to cool. Check the lids by pressing them with the finger. In case some of the jars with the pear orange jam are unsealed, place them into the fridge or reprocess the unsealed jars.

Nutritional Information (1 tbsp):

Calories: 61; Total fat: 3 oz; Total carbohydrates: 18 oz; Protein: 4 oz

# Pineapple-Apple Jam

*Prep Time: 40 min.│Makes around 5 10 oz jars*

Ingredients:

10 big and sweet Fuji apples, peeled and cubed

1 pineapple, cubed

5 cups of sugar

3 tsp. vanilla

2 tsp. citric acid

How to Prepare:

1. Wash and peel the Fuji apples and then cube them. Spoon the sugar and citric acid over the apples and pineapple. Set aside for around 1 to 2 hours unrefrigerated at room temperature or place in the fridge for overnight.

2. Boil the apples and pineapples with the sugar over medium heat for around 40 minutes, stirring all the time.

3. Few minutes before the apple jam is ready mix in the vanilla. Remove the saucepan from the heat and ladle freshly cooked jam into sterilized jars up to 1/5 inch from the top.

4. Flip the jars with the vanilla apple jam upside down or boil for around 10 minutes and then leave to cool. Check the lids by pressing them with the finger. In case some of the jars with the vanilla apple jam are unsealed, place them into the fridge or reprocess the unsealed jars.

Nutritional Information (1 tbsp):

Calories: 46; Total fat: 2 oz; Total carbohydrates: 11 oz; Protein: 3 oz

# Baked Pumpkin-Orange Jam

*Prep Time: 50 min. | Makes around 7 11 oz jars*

Ingredients:

2 lb pumpkin, diced

1 lb oranges, diced

5 cups of sugar

2 tbsp. orange zest, minced

1 cup of orange juice

1 tbsp. cinnamon

baking spray or butter

How to Prepare:

1. Spoon the sugar and pour one cup of the orange juice over the pumpkin and then set aside for around 1 to 3 hours unrefrigerated at room temperature.

2. Preheat the oven to 300°-350° Fahrenheit and then coat the baking pan with the baking spray or butter.

3. Spoon the cinnamon and orange zest over the pumpkin. Then bake the pumpkin with the sugar, orange juice, oranges and cinnamon for around 50 minutes until thickened and gelled enough, if not gelled enough continue baking and testing every five to ten minutes. The pumpkin and orange jam should be gelled enough to spoon it into the jars.

4. When the apple orange jam is ready spoon the freshly baked jam into the sterilized and hot jars up to 1/5 inch from the top and then seal the jars.

5. Flip the jars upside down or boil for around 10 minutes and then leave to cool. Check the lids by pressing them with the finger. In case some of the jars with the jam are unsealed, place them into the fridge or reprocess the unsealed jars.

Nutritional Information (1 tbsp):

Calories: 51; Total fat: 1 oz; Total carbohydrates: 11 oz; Protein: 2 oz

# Strawberry-Apple Jam

---

*Prep Time: 40 min.│Makes around 4 10 oz jars*

---

Ingredients:

8 big and sweet Gala apples, peeled and cubed

2 lb strawberries

5 cups of sugar

2 tsp. Cinnamon

2 tsp. citric acid

How to Prepare:

1. Wash and peel the apples and then cube them. Spoon the sugar and citric acid over the apples and set aside for around 3 to 4 hours unrefrigerated at room temperature or place in the fridge for overnight.

2. Boil the apples and strawberries with the sugar over medium heat for around 40 minutes, stirring all the time.

3. Few minutes before the apple jam is ready stir in the cinnamon. Remove the saucepan from the heat and ladle freshly cooked jam into sterilized jars up to 1/5 inch from the top.

4. Flip the jars with the apple jam upside down or boil for around 10 minutes and then leave to cool. Check the lids by pressing them with the finger. In case some of the jars with the apple jam are unsealed, place them into the fridge or reprocess the unsealed jars.

Nutritional Information (1 tbsp):
Calories: 46; Total fat: 4 oz; Total carbohydrates: 8 oz; Protein: 2 oz

# Orange Apricot Jam

---

*Prep Time: 40 min.│Makes around 6 10 oz jars*

---

Ingredients:

4 lb apricots, peeled and sliced

5 cups of sugar

2 tsp. orange zest, minced

4 tbsp. orange juice

How to Prepare:

1. Boil the apricots with the sugar over medium heat for around 40 minutes, stirring all the time until the sugar dissolves. Remove the foam from the surface.

2. Pour some jam on a plate and check if it has gelled enough, by pressing with the finger, if not continue boiling and testing every five or ten minutes. The jam should be thick enough to spoon it into the jars. Few minutes before the jam is ready mix in the orange zest and orange juice and keep stirring. When the jam is ready, remove the saucepan from the heat and ladle freshly cooked jam into the sterilized jars up to 1/5 inch from the top and seal the jars.

3. Flip the jars with the jam upside down or process them in a water bath. In a large pot, boil the jars for around 10 minutes and then take them out and leave to cool. Check the lids by pressing them with the finger. In case some of the jars with the jam are unsealed, place them into the fridge or reprocess the unsealed jars.

Nutritional Information (1 tbsp):
Calories: 54; Total fat: 2 oz; Total carbohydrates: 12 oz; Protein: 2 oz

# Conclusion

Thank you for buying this homemade jams and jellies cookbook. I hope this cookbook was able to help you to prepare delicious fruit jams or jellies recipes.

**If you've enjoyed this book, I'd greatly appreciate if you could leave an honest review on Amazon.**

Reviews are very important to us authors, and it only takes a minute for you to post.

Your direct feedback could be used to help other readers to discover the advantages of jams and jellies!

Thank you again and I hope you have enjoyed this cookbook.

Made in United States
Troutdale, OR
07/23/2023

11509165R00139